PIVOT POINTS

PIVOT POINTS

Creating A Culture Of Preparedness And Resiliency In America

Paul T Martin

ISBN: 1515310671
ISBN 13: 9781515310679
Library of Congress Control Number: 2015912500
CreateSpace Independent Publishing Platform
North Charleston, South Carolina

TABLE OF CONTENTS

For my parents, Doc and Pat:
Although you never thought of yourselves as preppers, the life lessons you instilled in us
clearly led me down this path. And for that, I am very grateful.

ACKNOWLEDGEMENTS

You would think that publishing one book would make the second one easier. For me, that certainly wasn't the case.

A number of people provided tremendous guidance and assistance in helping me put these thoughts together. I am grateful for their help.

My wife, Kendel, who gets to listen to me talk about this subject matter far more than she would like, has always been a great supporter of my writing efforts. Her support and proofreading have been invaluable.

Her sister, Kristin Bailey, Ph.D., lent her writing and editing skills to this project, as she did with my first book. Her guidance and suggestions can be found throughout the following pages. I appreciate not only her time but also her candor and counsel.

There are a number of people who granted me permission to quote them or use their materials in my efforts to make the case for building the culture of preparedness. Their willingness to share their thoughts clearly improved the quality of my work.

INTRODUCTION

This book is an open letter to those in the preparedness movement. It's also a letter to those who have a servant heart and want to see America build stronger communities.

Preparedness makes for a weird passion. And while I suppose there are quirkier hobbies, no one gets into preparedness because it seems like a fun way to spend time. You get into preparedness because you think your world may go to hell.

Writing about preparedness has helped me get better prepared. It's also given me a front row seat to observe the nuances of the preparedness culture. For years, I've felt the urge to talk about preparedness in a way that transcends the usual "buy some guns and MREs (meals, ready to eat) and cloister yourself from the rest of society" books we see on the subject.

I tried blogging, but it never let me drill down into the subject matter adequately. One day, I came across a video by Jack Canfield, author of the book *Chicken Soup For The Soul*. He made a very interesting observation, urging viewers to write the book they've been searching for.[1] That really resonated with me, because I wasn't finding the kind of books I was seeking in the preparedness genre. And so I began writing. Actually, I began dictating, just stream of consciousness kind of material, hoping that I could somehow organize it into chapters and something more meaningful to readers.

As I collected these thoughts in writing, I realized my attitude about preparedness has changed, rather radically in some ways. For years, I believed that preppers (a name for those in the preparedness movement) should primarily focus on their own well-being, allowing the rest of society to fend for itself. My attitude stemmed from the negative portrayal preppers receive from popular culture and main stream media. It's hard for many of us to talk about our interest in this subject with non-preppers, lest we be ridiculed or accused of being mentally unstable.

Much to my surprise, my new message challenged my old, selfish mindset. I found I no longer believed the preparedness movement has the time or luxury to keep our motivations and knowledge to ourselves. We cannot worry about what others may think of our preparedness efforts. We need more people joining us sooner, rather than later; staying in the closet does nothing to make our communities and families more resilient.

As a beta test of this newly found message, I spoke at a preparedness conference in January 2015, calling on attendees to help build a culture of preparedness in America. I wanted to see how well the message would resonate with fellow preppers. During a break after the presentation, two attendees approached me – separately – and asked me a poignant question:

> *"What caused you to change your attitude about the need for preppers to go out and create a culture of preparedness?"*

I was floored. In all of my planning, thinking, researching and writing, I could not believe I had never thought to ask myself that critical question. More troubling, I quickly surmised I didn't have an answer for them. My mindset had evolved over time, a function of life experiences, spiritual development and study of the current state of national readiness. There was no event on the road to Damascus or flaming bush. There was no Jerry McGuire moment.

Yet somewhere along the way, I clearly pivoted in my thought process. I realized the course I was on wasn't that helpful in the bigger scheme of things. It seemed wasteful of time, talent and energy for preppers to keep saying and doing the same things with some hope that people would join us in our efforts.

The idea of staying the course no longer appealed to me. I realized our movement needs to be on a different course – one where those in the movement are out in the community, helping others, setting a good example, being charitable, demonstrating good citizenship, and effectuating a culture change to incorporate preparedness strategies in our lives.

I tried to determine the exact moment I pivoted. It frustrated me that I couldn't pinpoint that mile marker when I went from an "*I'm going to be ready and you're not*" mindset to one of "*preppers need to be leading the effort to get others to do the same.*" Eventually it occurred to me: it doesn't matter what my pivot point was. Everyone is going to have a different pivot point, at which they will begin to make preparedness a priority in their lives. Some will pivot towards preparedness because of their parental instincts. Some will do so because the tenets of their faith will call them to be prepared. Others will do so in order to be in a better position to help people in need. Our job is to become apostles in the movement and help people find their own pivot points.

I gave a talk about the preparedness culture to the students and faculty of my high school a few years ago. One of the students asked me if I believed in the zombie apocalypse (ZA). For those of you who aren't familiar with this subculture of preppers, there are people who claim they are taking steps to ready themselves for the possibility (some might say the inevitability) of half dead people roaming the earth, looking to eat/infect/kill/maim healthy human beings. I personally think most of those who embrace the ZA culture know such a scenario won't actually happen and instead think of the ZA more in a metaphorical context. The "zombies" they fear really aren't undead beings roaming around; they are a host of perils - severe weather, civil unrest, pandemics and economic crises to name a few.

I responded to the young man's question by telling him that while I don't fear zombies, if someone feels the need to better prepare themselves for an actual zombie attack, they should do so. If that's what it takes to get them better prepared to handle a variety of emergencies, then by all means they should prepare themselves for zombies. I'm not so focused on why we get there. I'm focused on getting more people engaging in a culture of preparedness for whatever reason that's motivating them.

Our movement needs a course correction. We need to pivot towards a path that will positively change the country. We also need to avoid the temptation of judging the pivot points of others, instead appreciating the fact they found a pivot point that resonated with them.

Because I've changed course and am urging those in the preparedness movement to consider doing the same, I should inoculate you before moving forward. Much of what I'm going to tell you in this book is common sense. I'm telling you this now, as a way to prepare you against thinking these are new ideas and concepts. The ideas I will share with you are not radical, as most of them have been around for ages. We've simply forgotten them or made them less important over time.

There's also a fair amount of tough love and criticism of many in the preparedness movement in the pages to come. Rest assured my message comes from the heart, one prepper to another, in an effort to get all of us working in a more productive direction. Not too long ago, I held the very mindset that I am criticizing in this book. Some of the ideas and perhaps even entire chapters may bother you.

I'll tell you up front: I am going to talk about God, guns, citizenship, charity and politics from time to time. On occasion, I will be critical of certain government actions and policies. I don't say that to turn you off. I'm giving you permission to skip those parts and to vehemently disagree with me. Know that we don't have to agree on everything in order to build a culture of preparedness in America.

I do not harbor any illusions that this book will change the world. However, I do think that when it comes to things for which we are passionate, some of us are called to be change agents and contributors to the body of work surrounding that passion. It's my hope that by sharing this message, those in our movement will begin to take action and help others find their pivot points towards preparedness as well.

Some will no doubt criticize my ideas. If they do, it means people are reading the book and debating the central issue I pose throughout: the need to create a culture of preparedness in America. I welcome the criticism and debate, not because I relish conflict, but because I understand such discussions are necessary to advance the cause I promote.

Thank you for hearing me out.

Paul Martin
Austin, Texas
September 2015

DARK

MIDNIGHT, SUNDAY, FEBRUARY 16, 1986.

I spent that Saturday in Nashville, an hour's drive from our country home outside of Bell Buckle, Tennessee, at a 4-H Club speech contest. I turned sixteen years old just weeks earlier. I had gone to bed an hour before, but I was still awake listening to AM radio. Most likely, one of my favorite stations – WBBM 780 out of Chicago - would have faded in and out of reception on the AM/FM/weather band radio I kept by my bed. I started listing to WBBM as a kid, as they ran an all-news format 24 hours a day. Even though I had little interest in local Chicago news, I found it interesting to listen to high-quality news programming. Knowing things – having information and knowledge – gave me a sense of control over my own destiny.

Around midnight, the phone rang. It's rare that one receives good news at that hour, and this was no exception. Roughly a minute later, I heard my dad's car start up and race down the long driveway on the hill where our house looked out over hundreds of square miles of Middle Tennessee. I got out of bed and stepped down the hall towards the kitchen. I stopped dead in my tracks to hear my mother talking on the phone, with obvious stress in her voice: "*There is a fire at the FranceWillard residence on Ebb Joyce Road in Deason.*"

The adrenaline hit hard and fast. I knew I was supposed to be in bed, but I quickly went down the hall towards my mother, who was fumbling for keys to the truck. "I'm going with you," I announced, hoping she wouldn't insist that I stay at the house with my younger brother. I suppose being sixteen the time, my mother felt I was responsible enough to be of some assistance.

I grabbed my coveralls and boots and ran towards the truck. I remember my mom running up to the truck and looking off in the distance, down the hill towards where the Willards' house sat. The fear and sadness in her voice were apparent. "*Oh God! Oh God!*" she kept saying over and over, distressed to see (as I was) the warm, beautiful glow of an orange and yellow light emanating from the woods below our house. Warm, yet deadly. Beautiful, yet destructive.

I threw my outer gear into the bed of the truck, quickly jumping onto the truck's rear tire to climb back there as well. As my mother fired up the engine and raced down the hill from the house, I put on my coveralls and boots while standing in the truck bed, paying little attention to the cold Tennessee air that February night.

The Willards were our closest neighbors, and yet they were still a good half a mile away. France Willard had passed away a number of years earlier; Mrs. Willard had lived in the house as a widow for some time.

They were fantastic neighbors. I called Mr. France one night when my parents were out of town. I had noticed people trespassing at our pond, betrayed by the flashlights they were holding as they went frog gigging one spring evening. France took off after them, got the license plate of the trespasser's vehicle and came back to the house. I invited him inside to be with me when I called the county sheriff to give the license plate number. I remember hanging up the phone with the sheriff's department, only to have him say "What I should've done is put several rounds into the pond with my hunting rifle. That would really scare them!"

I knew he wasn't kidding. A few years before that, he caught someone breaking into his barn stealing his gas. He opened fire on the thief, later telling my father, "I don't know if I hit him or the tree he was standing next to." One thing was for sure: you did not mess with France Willard.

Less than a minute after leaving our house, my mom raced the truck down the long driveway of the Willards. Roughly one third of the home was fully involved in fire this point. The house, which was several decades old, was no match for the growing conflagration. Mom skidded the truck to a stop, and I jumped out, looking for Dad. I got almost completely around the house when I heard my own name being yelled back at me. Dad was taking furniture out of the bedroom as best he could. I remember looking at the furniture and being amazed that he was able to get all that out by himself.

"Help me get this furniture out!" he shouted, making it clear by his tone of voice that he was quite concerned for his own safety. We went inside the smoky house; to this day I remember the smell of the smoke burning my eyes and throat. Dad and I picked up a dresser, drawers and all, and moved it out of the house. I remember thinking: *this has to be one of the heaviest things I've ever carried in my life.* On one of his last trips inside, Dad found Mrs. Willard's dog, sitting in a chair. He gently picked it up and brought it to safety.

Dad and I did what we could to help the firefighters. We didn't have any training, but we could help move things from time to time. At one point, the fire chief reported they were putting over 2,000 gallons of water every minute on the house, but that they were afraid to use more water than that. The structure simply could not sustain more water pressure being applied to the fire. Within the next twenty or thirty minutes, the old house was reduced to a pile of hot embers.

As the night wore on, France Willard's legacy came back to visit us one more time. He was a big believer in having a loaded gun by every door. As the fire went on, the ammunition began to cook off. We regularly heard rounds whizzing over our heads.

The sights, sounds, and the smells of that evening some 30 years ago are still with me as if it happened last night. Those events helped put me on a journey to be better prepared to deal with emergencies. Years later, fulfilling a promise I made to myself that evening, I joined a local volunteer fire department. I learned a tremendous amount working in the fire service, even as a volunteer.

Throughout the years, my interest in disasters, as well as weather, geopolitics, economics, firearms, agriculture and self-defense seemed to culminate into a rather small but well defined spot on a Venn diagram. This sweet spot has been named different things over the years, but today we call those individuals "preppers." People have differing opinions as to what makes someone a prepper; suffice it to say we are all interested in preparing ourselves to deal with crises in our communities.

My survival experiences did not end there. At the beginning of my sopho-more year of college, I began experiencing intense abdominal pain — the worst I'd ever experienced in my life. After my very first colonoscopy, I was diagnosed with ulcerative colitis at the ripe old age of 19. I had no idea what ulcerative coli-tis was. I just assumed the doctor would give me some pills and that the problem would go away. My doctor quickly dispelled that notion when he mentioned that those who do not get better invariably have to have a colostomy. That's not what a 19 year old wants to hear.

Given that prognosis, I hoped the medicine would make me better, and it did. Yet the side effects of the medication, along with their reduced efficacy over time, made my life quite unpleasant for a number of years. Despite the hor-rific side effects of such large doses of anti-inflammatory steroids, I managed to graduate from college and enroll in law school at the University of Miami.

When I arrived in Miami, I had precious little to my name and few survival supplies. I did have a small NOAA weather radio, a battery-powered AM/FM radio, and an oil fueled lamp that my mother sent with me "in case the power goes out because of a storm." My car overheated on the drive down the Florida peninsula, and so for several days after I arrived, it remained in the repair shop as I got around on foot and by hitching rides with newly made friends.

The local news reports that first week stated a hurricane had formed in the Atlantic but that all forecasts indicated would not impact South Florida. I picked up a copy of the Miami Herald and clipped out the little hurricane tracking chart from the weather section and taped it to my desk. I dutifully charted the course of the storm over the next several days, listening to my weather radio several times a day for updates. The updates became more frequent, and the news more urgent, during the week before school was to start. My first day of law school, however, would be delayed.

The school postponed the start of the semester as Hurricane Andrew came ashore near Homestead, Florida on August 24, 1992, killing 26 nationwide, and 15 in Florida alone.[2] To date, Andrew is the second costliest hurricane to hit the United States.[3]

A few days after the storm decimated the southern suburbs of Miami, I went back to the apartment complex to see what of my belongings still remained.

While the third floor – the top floor – of the apartment complex was damaged, the second floor where I lived was remarkably intact.

And it began. For 17 days, I had no electricity. Fortunately, the gas lines of the building still worked, so I could cook on the stove. Living in Miami in August with no electricity is fairly close to a third world experience. And because life wasn't challenging enough at that point, my colon teetered on the beginnings of a flare-up of ulcerative colitis. Good times.

To pass the time, I started making lists and notes about how to avoid a similar experience. I promised that I would never allow myself or my family to endure a storm or other disaster like that without basic preparations ever again. To help keep the students on track, the law school gave us some basic reading assignments. One night, I got out the oil lamp that mom had sent "just in case" and began reading the assignment in my torts class by lamplight. I remember sitting in my apartment without electricity, wearing nothing but a pair of shorts in an effort to cope with the 90 degree temperature and 90 percent humidity that was the typical August evening in Miami, reading a law book like Abraham Lincoln must've done 150 years earlier.

Eventually, the power came back on, school resumed, and Miami recovered. My health, on the other hand, was a different story. For another two years, I suffered through the disease and the side effects of medication. It was becoming apparent to me and many of my classmates during my second year of law school that my health was taking a turn for the worse. My 5'10" frame had dropped down to under 130 pounds, and I was losing muscle tone and mass rapidly. At the gym, I struggled to bicep curl 15 pound weights through 10 repetitions.

Perhaps the worst part of having ulcerative colitis was the constant emotional roller coaster I was on. I had much difficulty concentrating, became rather irritable at times, and struggled to maintain basic interpersonal relationships with friends and family. I had to be careful about going out socially, especially when my colitis was flaring up. Despite all that, I never felt sorry for myself. I don't say that because I am trying to brag or appear tougher than I am. Regardless of what my body was going through, I knew that the end of the day I had to plow through it. I had to get up, go to class, take notes, study, and do the best I could on exams. Stopping my education wasn't an option.

The symptoms intensified, and so in May 1994, a surgeon at the Mayo Clinic put me through a battery of tests right after the end of my second year of law school. After three days of being poked, prodded and violated, the good doctor gave me my treatment choices. The first was to switch to a cancer drug that was indicated for use in colitis patients. The other option was to have major reconstructive surgery of my colon. Tired of taking medications, I opted for the latter.

It was not until three months later, when all the anti-inflammatory drugs I'd been taking over the last five years finally left my system, I realized just how sick I had been. While the dark of the Tennessee woods at night never disturbed me, it was clear I'd been through my own personal dark period, far more disturbing and mentally draining than any nighttime stroll. For the first time in five years, I could think clearly. I had more self-esteem. I relaxed more. I had completely forgotten what it was like to be healthy; I had to re-learn what was normal.

And when we have such episodes in our lives, what is our response to it? Some let it get the best of them. Others power through it. A few ride out the storm, enjoying every minute of it. These periods of challenge and suffering often make us stronger people. As it says in the New Testament, suffering builds character, and character builds hope.[4] Do we ever harness that new character to do greater things, helping others? Or are we content to let it rest in our subconscious, running in the background of our mind's operating software?

I would submit to you that those experiences in the dark help enable us to survive bigger challenges. Those challenges can be very diverse in nature — personal setbacks, a job loss, or a catastrophic event in our lives. What if we harnessed what we learn in the darkness not only to help ourselves in the future, but also to help others avoid or cope with the dark themselves?

Being a public advocate for preparedness is a calling of sorts. This calling has no doubt been shaped by a number of experiences, including the fire at the Willards' house. The culmination of those experiences, my mental energy devoted to the subject, and my prior writings have resulted in this book. I hope to share with you why I am so passionate about this subject, as well as to start a conversation about three important questions:

1. Do we need a culture of preparedness in America?
2. If so, what would that culture look like?
3. And how would we go about creating it?

In the coming pages, I will make the case that we should think about preparedness not as a hobby or a trait of a quirky personality, but instead think of it as a means to strengthen our nation, protect our people, and learn about the bigger world around us in the process.

But first, is the current preparedness movement even succeeding?

PIVOT POINTS:

- Events and crises in our daily lives may be the best motivators for people to inculcate a preparedness culture into their homes and with their families.
- If you are looking for a good civic opportunity in which to share your time and talent, consider becoming an apostle of the preparedness movement in your community.

FAIL

The preparedness movement in America has failed.

You would not know that by reading various publications devoted to the subject. A quick Internet search will yield hundreds of articles reporting on the growing preparedness movement in America. Americans from all walks of life – white-collar, blue-collar, urban, rural, rich, poor, college-educated, high school dropouts – are preparing for some form of major disruption in our way of life. And to some extent, there is empirical evidence to prove people are beginning to prepare.

National Geographic commissioned a survey of 1,007 U.S. residents to determine their various attitudes towards preparedness.[5] To those who monitor the preparedness movement, many of the results were not surprising. For example, 64 percent of those surveyed believe that the United States could be affected by a major earthquake in the next 25 years. Some 63 percent of those surveyed believe that America is susceptible to a major hurricane in that same time frame.

Other aspects of the survey, however, should give all Americans reason to explore our attitudes about the future. For example, 51 percent of those surveyed felt a financial collapse of the United States economy was likely in the next 25 years. Given that, it should come as no surprise that 41 percent of survey participants believe that making disaster preparations – such as a bomb shelter – is a better investment for the future than putting money into a 401(k). Think about that for a moment: two out of every five Americans would rather put money into canned food, barrels of water, stockpiles of first aid supplies and a bombproof room in their house than to invest money in more traditional assets, such as stocks and bonds. Ten years ago, such a prevalent mindset would be incomprehensible.

The Federal Emergency Management Agency (FEMA) completed its own study on the state of readiness of Americans. In July 2013, FEMA released "Personal Preparedness in America: Findings From the 2012 FEMA National Survey." Some of the highlights from that survey include:

- Some 31 percent of those interviewed said they had discussed preparedness with others.
- For those Americans receiving information about preparedness, 55 percent of them took steps to prepare.
- More than half of those responding to the survey have disaster supplies in their home.[6]

On its face, it appears that the preparedness movement is in fact succeeding quite nicely. One would not expect such survey results if Americans were not becoming more attuned to the need to be ready for emergencies. But is that really accurate?

HOW DID WE GET HERE?

The history of the modern-day preparedness movement has its roots in the Cold War. The fear of a nuclear conflagration with the Soviet Union motivated many people to build bomb shelters and stockpile food and water. Invariably, the fear subsided as the Berlin Wall came down. The food stores either were eaten or went bad. Bomb shelters became game rooms and storage areas.

The oil shocks and inflation of the 1970s created additional fears to the Cold War boogeyman. Preppers (or *retreaters* as they were often called during this era) made plans to be more self-sufficient in anticipation of rampant inflation destroying the U.S. economy. Yet when the economy began rebounding in the 1980s, inflation dipped below three percent in 1983. The specter of economic collapse seemed a distant threat; the perceived need to prepare for trouble subsided.

Then Y2K came along. Old software programs, lacking the ability to recognize the truncated notation for the year 2000, caused grave concerns among many who maintained the supervisory control and data acquisition (SCADA) networks running many of the utility providers and banking systems around the world. In the days leading up to January 1, 2000, worries of a computer induced societal meltdown abated rather quickly. The portable generators, guns, MREs, and various survival products purchased for Y2K were stored away in closets or sold secondhand.

These things never came to fruition, despite dire warnings from many. Perhaps the failure of these events to come to pass lulled us into a false sense of security.

This false sense of security evaporated when the September 11 attacks brought terrorism to the doorstep of the United States. Of course, many could argue that terrorism came some six years earlier when Timothy McVeigh conspired to blow up the federal building in Oklahoma City. Others might argue that the 1996 Olympic Park bombing marked the beginning of modern-day terrorism in the United States. It matters little which event one chooses to mark the beginning of a new era in our country; the National Geographic survey reveals that 51% of Americans feel they are unprepared for another disaster like terrorism.

Fast forward to 2005. Hurricane Katrina made landfall along the Gulf Coast of the United States. In its wake, over 1,800 people died. The city of New Orleans filled with feet of water. Refugees were trapped in the Superdome for days without power. The United States Coast Guard rescued hundreds of people from water swollen streets and rooftops throughout the city.

Four years later, Hurricane Ike made landfall on the Gulf Coast near Houston. Official tallies credit Ike with killing dozens of people and costing $24.9 billion in damage, suggesting it was the third most expensive hurricane to affect the United States.[7] Hurricane Sandy came ashore in 2012 in the northeastern United States. In New York City - one of the most affluent cities on the planet - people were dumpster diving for food within days of the storm.[8]

The financial markets brought us a new kind of disaster in 2008. Fueled by easy credit and lax lending guidelines, mortgage lenders made large volumes of loans to people unable to repay them. As these loans started to sour, the American financial markets cratered; the S&P 500 lost roughly 57% of its value over an eighteen month timeframe. With this financial meltdown, unemployment in the United States went from 4.7% in October 2007 to 10% in October 2009. As of July 2015, unemployment had not returned to pre-recession levels, to say nothing of the long-term unemployed, whose lives have truly been completely turned upside down, perhaps irrevocably.

And yet people claim the preparedness movement is succeeding.

If it is, then why aren't we better prepared for hurricanes and terrorism? If it is, why are those who call themselves "preppers" still viewed as part of a lunatic fringe, portrayed as a group of people who hope and pray they get to use their AR-15 rifles in shoot outs with their neighbors, snacking on freeze dried ice cream sandwiches in between fire fights? Even National Geographic's television show entitled "Doomsday Preppers" is part of a series the network calls "American Outliers," implying that those who are preparing for harder times are not in the main stream culture of America. Our government and various non-government organizations (NGOs) encourage people to prepare....yet those who do are chastised by many in the main stream media as uneducated and unwashed. With all the purported concern about a variety of foreseeable calamities, 51% of Americans responding to the National Geographic survey indicate they are not as prepared as they need to be for a potential disaster.

In the days after Hurricane Katrina, Time Magazine ran an article entitled "Why We Don't Prepare."[9] The author drives home a sad yet accurate point: despite the fact we know bad things will happen, our lack of ambition, forethought, perseverance, and plain old grit, the typical American fails to take meaningful steps to prepare for the most basic emergencies.

The preparedness movement in America has failed. But it's not because people aren't interested in preparing. It's because we have failed to create a culture of preparedness in America, in which citizens appreciate the benefits of preparedness even when the bad things don't happen on the assumed time table. *"It won't happen to me/here/anytime soon"* has become our de facto national preparedness plan, despite the efforts of the government and NGOs. The willingness to prepare has fallen into a state of disrepair, harbored only by those old enough to remember harder times and those currently making the effort to prepare for the possibility those hard times can happen again.

The Role of FEMA and Non-Government Organizations

I suspect many Americans think we have outsourced our preparedness responsibilities to the government and to disaster relief agencies. When a major disaster strikes our country, the Federal Emergency Management Agency (FEMA) and various non-government organizations activate various response teams in the affected areas to provide material and financial aid, as well as counseling, to those affected. State and local governments, along with local NGOs, do so as well.

These organizations have made significant efforts to get you and me better prepared for the possibility of a disaster. Consider FEMA's "Are You Ready?" initiative. The agency has undertaken a significant public relations campaign and provides resources on its website to help people prepare their homes and businesses for a wide spectrum of perils. It partners with community groups to help get the word out. NGOs undertake similar efforts, partnering with local chapters and other community groups to teach people not only how to be prepared for disasters but also how to deal with various medical emergencies. Make no mistake - if all of us undertook the effort to do the bare minimums recommended by these organizations, our nation would be much more resilient.

Yet most Americans seem woefully unprepared for the basic emergencies they may face. While FEMA and NGOs may be making progress, Americans are not taking their advice often enough.

Why The Failure To Create The Culture?

I suspect one of the reasons we fail to prepare is the preparedness movement itself. Many leaders within the movement, for many of whom I have a deep respect, believe the best preparedness strategy is to unplug from the grid, move out to the country, and become a homesteader.[10]

Homesteading can certainly be a challenging and very rewarding lifestyle for the people who choose it; yet your typical suburban family isn't going to do that. In fact, empirical evidence shows the rate of migration from urban and suburban areas to rural areas slowed dramatically last decade.[11] They would rather continue to live their lives, complete with easy access to well-paying jobs, good schools and medical care, and yes, also to pleasures like youth activities, good restaurants, and shopping. Even my own family has opted to remain in suburbia for these reasons. I suspect when a suburbanite picks up a book on preparedness strategies and invariably learns that the "best" strategy is to move out into the country and begin growing your own food and making your own clothes, the desire to become better prepared wanes exponentially.

The catalog of preparedness books and treatises contains precious few works regarding strategies on building an effective preparedness plan in a suburban or urban area. And those few works that do assume the reader is already motivated to get prepared; the ones I have read do not address how we can reach those skeptics who intellectually understand the benefits of preparing for emergencies but who perceive prepping to be daunting, expensive, or perhaps fanciful.

And then there are those in the movement who inadvertently perpetuate the negative stereotypes assigned to preparedness advocates. Our movement struggles in large part because we lack publicly visible leaders who promote practical preparedness. This shortage of leaders means the default spokespeople are the ones depicted on reality television shows. While there's nothing wrong about being a prepper on these shows *per se*, many of these individuals do not demonstrate preparedness strategies and attitudes that are sustainable or realistic for the average American to adopt.

We don't need more books on how to prepare. We need more exploration of how to build a culture of preparedness. And we need committed people to lead the way.

COULD WE HAVE FORESEEN THE FAILURE?

Was such a failure to create a preparedness culture, despite the disasters we've endured, predictable? Perhaps. We mistakenly believed an increased reliance on technology, to the diminution of reliance upon self-sufficiency, could not have been detrimental to our nation. Our error, made with the best intentions, was in assuming that with certain technological advances, we were essentially immune from various hardships that our parents and grandparents faced just a few years earlier.

Such an error is quite understandable. When we think about the technological advances over the last several decades which have made our lives better – medical breakthroughs, rural electrification, the Internet, flood control measures, advances in automobile safety, personal computers – it is easy to see how our nation could be lulled into a false sense of security. Despite the regular reminders of how susceptible our society is to storms and economic downturns, we quickly put those events into the past of our collective psyche, no doubt because there are always new and better distractions to occupy our time.

To build a culture of preparedness, we must understand how our attitudes towards self-sufficiency have changed since our parents and grandparents endured the Great Depression, World War II, and the constant threats of the Cold War. In short, our technological advances have created disincentives for us to be able to do for ourselves. Make no mistake: I am not immune from the side effects of such advances. I have much to learn to become more self-sufficient. That's a big part of the battle we will fight in developing a new culture of preparedness in America: convincing others how technology and modern conveniences can fail us in a crisis.

But there's a bigger battle we must wage first: are those of us in the movement just a bunch of crazy heads?

PIVOT POINTS:

- While a fair number of people are taking action to prepare, there are far too many who aren't. Frequent news stories of people who aren't prepared for an oncoming storm or other disaster prove this.

- Building the culture of preparedness means we need to be willing to create viable strategies for people where they live.
- Articulating the side effects of technological advancements – the loss of self-reliance and resilience – is critical when explaining to others the need to be better prepared.

NUT JOB

Are preppers nuts?

Make no mistake: there are people who take prepping to such an extreme that reasonable people could conclude they suffer from a mental illness. Those who isolate themselves from the world to the point they have a hard time functioning in a meaningful way may in fact need the services of a mental health professional.

But that's not to say that everyone who sets aside food and water for long-term storage or puts an emergency backpack in their vehicle needs to be tagged with a diagnosis of paranoia. Having a ham radio and an AR-15 rifle are not symptoms of a mental illness. Nor is taking a bearish view of global finance and central banks. Meanwhile, reality television shows seek out individuals who have taken extraordinary measures to be prepared for a wide spectrum of perils. If the typical viewer has no impression of prepping other than what they see on such a show, it's easy to see why many in the public think preppers are nut jobs.

And even when the mainstream media portrays preppers as being somewhat enlightened, it's done so in a backhanded compliment, proclaiming that preppers are focused primarily on some sort of doomsday event.[12] The notion that preppers are only concerned about being self-sufficient for the apocalypse serves as a signal to the rest of us: even when we are portrayed as being insightful, it's only because we are allegedly obsessed about a full bore collapse of society. You will note that those who take steps to prepare for crises are never portrayed as doing so to handle the more common emergencies, such as power outages, wildfires, injuries around the home and severe weather events.

Much of today's conventional wisdom, including global diagnoses of all preppers as being mentally unstable, is wrong. In his book, *The Half-Life of Facts: Why Everything We Know Has an Expiration Date*, Samuel Arbesman argues that half of what we know right now will be determined to be incorrect or obsolete in just a few years.[13] For example, he postulates that the half- life of knowledge on medical conditions such as cirrhosis and hepatitis is approximately 45 years.[14] If we were apply that same conclusion to what the public knows about the preparedness movement, Arbesman's sobering claim has important implications; namely, the so called "facts" about prepping and those who engaged in the practice the year I was born are now reaching their half-life. Again assuming the half-life for facts about preppers is the same as it is for cirrhosis and hepatitis just for the sake of discussion (and with the full understanding that the accuracy of all current knowledge doesn't deteriorate precisely on a true half-life schedule), the "facts that everyone knows" about the psychological health of preppers during the Y2K/September 11 era have already decayed approximately 21% as of the writing of this book.[15] I would submit a 21% error rate is significant enough to raise skepticism in the minds of intellectually honest people about what they truly know and understand about those who make readiness a priority.

How can I make the claim that those who take preparedness seriously aren't laboring under some sort of mental illness? Because some psychology experts believe preparing for a disaster is a means of *improving* our nation's mental health and sense of community.

THE LESSONS OF MAYAN VILLAS

Jane Sinagub, Ph.D., completed her graduate work in psychology at the University of Miami. But before she was Dr. Sinagub, to me she was simply Jane, graduate student and fiance' of Paul Ranis — my best friend in law school.

The three of us lived in Mayan Villas, a South Miami apartment complex near the U.M. campus. We began our graduate work in August 1992 — Ranis and I in law school, and Jane in a master's program for her psychology degree. We met days after Hurricane Andrew ravaged our apartment complex. And yet we were lucky — some of our classmates and professors lost far more.

Pensive with a razor-sharp intellect, when Dr. Sinagub speaks, she has something of merit to say. Although her expertise is not in the area of the psychological aspects of disaster preparedness, having been through Hurricane Andrew, I knew she would have some guidance that would be helpful to me. And so I posed this question to her: *At what point does someone's disaster preparedness efforts become a symptom of a mental illness?*

When people close to you see your thoughts and/or actions are negatively impacting your quality of life, then that's usually a warning sign of a mental illness. So if your disaster preparedness actions get in the way with you holding down a job or having relationships, that's when we have a problem. If your disaster preparedness cognitions (like not leaving the house when it rains for fear of a tornado) impact your work or relationships, then it is a problem.

What keeps coming to my mind with regard to this area is that if you (or your life) become the disaster that you are trying to prepare for then you have failed, and you have a problem. Disaster preparedness is about avoiding and ameliorating disaster. If you turn your life into a disaster in the process, then you have failed. The people with true hard core mental illness won't see how they have ruined their lives, but everyday folks will see the toll it has taken at least once confronted with the reality.[16]

She makes an interesting observation: if your preparedness efforts are themselves a disaster (to the point that you cannot function normally with family, friends and coworkers), you've become what you fear. And that makes sense to us, as we see people in the media who have taken their preparations to such an extent that you wonder how they are able to hold down a job or have any meaningful relationship with their family. The fact someone is making preparedness a priority is not by itself evidence of some sort of mental issue. It's when we take such efforts to an extreme that psychological professionals began to take note of a potential problem.

READINESS AS A MEANS TO
PSYCHOLOGICAL WELLNESS

Matt "Disasterman" Davis, Ph.D. is not your typical psychology professor. Few in academia have done more than this tenured member of the psychology department at Dominican University of California to document the psychological implications of disaster preparedness. His nickname stems from his extensive work in the field of this unique specialty.

Davis' work focuses on public perceptions and the psychological implications of volcanoes and tsunamis. More recently, he's studied the effects of participation in disaster preparedness programs on psychological health. His work makes him a great resource in understanding this necessary topic.

Many preppers attribute the public's reluctance to get prepared to a sense of denial, believing the general population simply doesn't think something bad can happen. Davis challenges that belief, theorizing that such behavior is not based in denial, but rather in a lack of saliency.

> Denial, in the classic Freudian way of defining it, is when someone literally denies the possibility that something could happen to them, or something that has already happened to them because it is too much to cope with psychologically. Someone discovers a lump in their breast or testicle, and a denial response would be "it's nothing; it'll go away," because we're too afraid to cope with it, at least for the moment. Someone loses the ability to walk or to see because of an accident and may go into denial by refusing to believe or acknowledge what happened. In these cases, it's usually a rather short-lived response that gives us time to process what has happened. But this type of denial would lead to inaction dealing with the issue.[17]

So how does saliency come into play? Davis explains as follows:

> If something is low in *salience*, it means that it is not a noticeable or obvious aspect of our environment. It's not on our radar; it's not on the front

burner. With disasters, the folks I studied [living near the dangerous volcano Mount] Vesuvius cannot ignore the fact that they live under and beside the cone [of an active volcano], but the everyday issues of traffic, crowding, and petty crime are taking the majority of their attention.

If you ask someone, "What are the problems facing your city?" they will report the things that are most salient at that moment: traffic, political corruption, crime, poor public services. The fact that they don't mention Vesuvius as a problem is not indicative of them being in denial of the risk… it just means that compared to all these everyday issues, Vesuvius has left them alone since 1944. When I then asked them directly whether they thought Vesuvius posed a threat, the vast majority acknowledged that yes, it was and that they were afraid of an eruption. That is not denial… just a lack of salience.[18]

This analysis challenges the conventional wisdom within the preparedness movement. When we declare that those who fail to prepare are in denial, we are in essence saying that the public at large cannot accept the possibility that something can happen. What Davis is telling us, however, is that they most certainly can appreciate the risk and are often very much aware of it. What they cannot do, it seems, is increase their amount of mental bandwidth to make it a priority.

That's not meant as a criticism of those who do not prepare. We all have our own value systems and priorities. To build a preparedness culture, we need to understand what derails people from taking action. If we accept Professor Davis' theory, it means our challenge isn't in educating others in the possibilities of what might happen. Our task will be in convincing the public to move prepping for problems up higher on their "to do" lists.

Assuming we can get people to make preparedness a priority, will their efforts be psychologically helpful or harmful to them? Are we creating more psychological harm if we successfully encourage people to follow the FEMA mantra of "make a kit and have a plan?" According to Davis,

A major factor in why people do not take actions is a lack of self-efficacy. This means that they feel there is nothing they can do to remedy that situation or that they lack the skills or ability to take action. Self-efficacy, or lack of it, is not a personality trait... it's situationally dependent. I have low self-efficacy regarding whether I could fix my car if it breaks down, but I have high self-efficacy regarding preparing a lecture for a community group. My self-efficacy could change if I took an auto mechanics course or if I was going in front of a group of experts that I suspect might be critical of me or know more than me.

What I have found is that taking disaster prep courses increases people's sense of self-efficacy... they begin to feel that there *is* something they can do or that they have the skills to start taking action. If you can increase self-efficacy, and salience of the problem, you can increase preparedness.

With more community-based programs, we seem to increase people's sense of community, which is another variable that is positively associated with preparedness. People who feel more of a bond to their community are more likely to get involved and to take precautionary actions. If you don't know or like your neighbors or don't trust community officials, it's unlikely you'll participate in strategies they recommend.[19]

In San Francisco, residents have begun to prove Davis correct. The city participates in the Resilient Cities program created by the Rockefeller Foundation.[20] Neighborhoods create their own disaster plans and disaster supply caches, so that they are not dependent on disaster relief agencies.[21] The result: neighborhoods are not only better prepared for disaster, but they also improve their sense of community.[22]

Now we're ready to answer the first key question I posed earlier: Should we make the effort to build a preparedness culture in America?

Pivot Points:

- The media often portrays people who are taking preparedness seriously as nut jobs. However, psychologists believe that being prepared is a good thing, and that being *psychologically prepared* is key to that.
- Preparedness is like any other activity — taken to an extreme, it can be unhealthy. That's especially true if it is interfering with your ability to hold our job or to maintain relationships with other people.
- The best way to get people to prepare is to increase their self-efficacy. Community training efforts — even ones that you create yourself — help with that.
- Preparedness not only benefits the individual; it improves the sense of community as well.

SHOULD WE?

S hould we build a culture of preparedness in America? Would it be harmful for us to improve our ability to handle a variety of crises? "Sure, why not?" might seem like the obvious answer to even the most apathetic soul. What could possibly go wrong?

I'm not convinced the answer is that simple. Creating the culture necessarily means we are changing the current culture. That often raises objections from those who oppose change. Don't get me wrong; few if any will openly say "I think it's a bad idea that people know first aid skills or have non-perishable food and water on hand for extended emergencies." Instead, they are likely to say "I'd rather not spend the time, money or effort to improve my level of preparedness, and I'd rather my charitable contributions not support such efforts, either." Or perhaps the objection is more fundamental: "I don't have the disposable income to do so." Some who are currently prepping might be the strongest critics of a culture change, lest an increase in demand for preparedness supplies drive up the price for them.

Let's walk step by step through some of the issues that need to be addressed in determining whether we should undertake the effort to create a preparedness culture.

WHAT IS A "CULTURE OF PREPAREDNESS?"

Think about the vast number of cultures and subcultures in America today: music, sports, outdoors, cooking, and fitness just to name a few. Some of these might be passing fads, while others have been ingrained into American society for centuries. But each represents a set of core interests, concerns and way of life for its members.

Those who would participate in the preparedness culture would have a set of common goals and concerns, too. People would not need prompting to prepare for storm season or the possibility of an economic downturn. Learning basic first aid and having extra food and water set aside for emergencies would become second nature. Enhanced building codes and disaster resistant upgrades in home construction would take their place alongside media rooms and granite counter tops. In short, all of us would get prepared without the need of a pending storm or terrorist attack to prod us into action.

Is it possible to create a culture of preparedness in America? Think about it this way. In my forty five years on Earth, we've become a nation of recyclers who are willing to re-think the criminality of marijuana and the prohibition of gay marriage. Interracial relationships, once taboo for many Americans, are now commonplace. The smoking rate has dropped from my childhood, when pregnant women smoked regularly, down to multi-decade lows today. Seat belt and bicycle helmet usage have become second nature since my childhood, when we never used either. Meanwhile, citizens having licenses to carry concealed handguns have become commonplace in most states, something that was unheard of just three decades ago.

Culture changes happen. The only thing preventing us from developing a culture of preparedness in America is our lack of action and knowledge on how to go about it. I would submit it is time we learn how and start making it happen.

WHAT WOULD A PREPAREDNESS CULTURE IN AMERICA LOOK LIKE?

The growing storm clouds on a warm spring day do not escape the attention of residents in a small town in Oklahoma. Weather radios in homes across the area provide the latest information on the worsening situation. Families have discussed and even rehearsed what they would do if a tornado hit their home, school, or while out driving around. Newer homes in the area have safe rooms built into them. Residents in older homes have made arrangements to seek shelter in reliable areas of safety. Some of the local youth, inspired by the disaster preparedness training they received at school, obtained their amateur radio or "ham" licenses and have been trained as area storm spotters; they will provide real time weather reporting to the National Weather Service to enable their forecasters to make better predictions. The storm doesn't materialize, fortunately, but stress levels are lower as people are confident their community has made the commitment to strengthen its storm readiness.

Families in Central Texas are not so lucky. Drought conditions continue to plague the area, causing massive wildfires throughout rural areas and green belted suburban areas. Residents learned their lessons from previous wildfires. Ordinances prohibiting the cutting of dried brush — originally enacted to preserve habitat for wildlife — have been revised to balance the need for disaster mitigation. Families have their important documents in fireproof boxes which they purchased from their local hardware stores. Homeowners and their insurance agents annually review their insurance coverages and discuss what's covered, how their deductibles are calculated, and whether the homeowner has enough coverage on their house. As fires go through neighborhoods, the impact is mitigated by the fact that brush was cleared, while gutters and roofs were kept free of leaves which might catch fire from flying hot embers. Some residents suffer minor injuries as they rushed their preparations to completion; other neighbors, who participated in a first aid class sponsored by their homeowner's association, provide initial medical treatment.

Meanwhile, a single mother living in Utah hears someone breaking into her home where her two small children are sleeping upstairs. To be prepared to defend herself and her family, she took a firearms safety class and learned how to use a handgun. Her training included a course that permits her to carry her gun concealed when she is out with her family. Getting her gun out of its dedicated lock box and taking a defensive position in her home as she has practiced, she yells to the intruder that she is armed and that she has called 911. Thinking twice about his prospects, the suspect runs away, leaving the mom and kids unharmed.

A family in upstate New York gets devastating news – the home's sole bread-winner has been laid off from work. With little job prospects any time soon, the family takes comfort knowing they have set aside a few months' worth of food and other consumables. They purchased a little extra every time they went grocery shopping, taking advantage of coupons and savings offered at discount warehouses. Times will be lean, but the family won't starve or go without necessities, thanks to their foresight.

A fire in a clothes dryer duct– a common origin of fires - of a home in suburban Chicago fills the halls with smoke in the early morning hours of a cold night. The three young women living there – renters, all of whom are college students – instinctively start communicating and working together to ensure they call 911 and get out of the house quickly. A smoke detector with a recently replaced battery alerted the sleeping women to the danger. They knew winter in Chicago was no time to be outside for prolonged periods in t-shirts and shorts, and so winter clothes were always nearby in case they needed to get out quickly. Their lives were likely saved by a nine volt battery inside of a ten dollar smoke detector.

These are some of the things we'd expect to see when a culture of preparedness becomes commonplace in America. And truth be told, there have been times in our nation's history when people were better prepared than they are today…meaning that our nation wouldn't be focusing on some new or controversial set of values. In short, preparedness should not be a hard sell.

WHAT WOULD BE THE DIRECT BENEFITS FROM HAVING SUCH A PREVALENT MINDSET IN AMERICA?

In short, having a national ethos of preparedness would save lives, property, and money.

Let's start with the most important of the three – the preservation of life. Consider the number of lives lost in 2010 due to some of the more common causes. The Center for Disease Control (CDC) determined in 2010, "fire departments responded to 384,000 home fires in the United States, which claimed the lives of 2,640 people …and injured another 13,350."[23] They also estimate 37 percent of deaths from house fires occur in homes lacking smoke detectors.[24] The leading cause of fire-related deaths, according to the CDC? Smoking.[25] Another major factor in residential house fire deaths is alcohol, the use of which contributes an estimated 40 percent to the death toll.[26]

Let's put that in perspective. If 37 percent of deaths occurred in homes without a working smoke detector, simple arithmetic tells us that would equate to about 977 deaths.[27] That means 977 mothers, fathers, sisters and brothers died in 2010 in a home without a ten dollar life safety device which could have greatly enhanced their chances of survival. If you could reduce the effects of smoking and alcohol in residential fire deaths, the annual death toll would drop even further.

The University Corporation for Atmospheric Research determined that flooding kills more than 100 people a year on average, making it the deadliest non-heat related weather hazard.[28] What's a common thread in flood deaths? Nearly half of these deaths stem from driving into areas where water covers the roadway.[29] Again, another perspective check: if we could get Americans to adhere to the "Turn Around, Don't Drown" slogan, we could cut flood deaths in nearly half.

Then there's CPR. According to the American Heart Association, CPR can double or triple the patient's odds of surviving a heart attack; yet only 32 percent of those patients receive CPR.[30] Allow that to sink in. We can radically increase the odds of our family members surviving a cardiac event by learning a simple chest compression technique. But in 68 percent of these cases, the victim receives no help.

Residents of Seattle are helping reverse that trend. King County, Washington boasts the best heart attack survival rates in the world, at a rate almost seven times higher than the national average.[31] The county also has the highest rate of bystander performed CPR, coupled with a financial commitment to provide additional training to local paramedics. The county government has created a "Shockingly Simple" program to register automated external defibrillator (AED) devices, allowing 911 dispatchers to direct bystanders to the nearest AED in an emergency.[32]   When people know CPR and have access to rescue tools like AEDs, life safety improves dramatically.

Even basic first aid skills, when properly taught, can save lives. Yet many lack the necessary skills to help themselves or others.   One British study revealed almost two thirds of Britons lack the basic first aid skills to help keep people alive during the most common emergencies.[33]

You get the point.   Despite these basic, inexpensive suggestions which would dramatically improve the outcomes of medical and trauma patients, our national narrative on the subject of protecting people from harm isn't about teaching basic safety or first aid. Instead, we are far more likely to worry about more dramatic, often violent, dangers, which garner a lot of press attention and generate fear but which are more far difficult to solve on both the societal and individual level. If we were truly concerned about preserving life, we'd be more focused on teaching people first aid skills and how to use a fire extinguisher – skills that could be useful in the kinds of emergencies that we are most likely to face.

Speaking of the top causes of death in America, can you guess the top ten?

1. Heart Disease
2. Cancer
3. Chronic lower respiratory diseases (like COPD)
4. Stroke
5. Accidents (unintentional injuries)
6. Alzheimer's disease
7. Diabetes
8. Kidney disease
9. Influenza and pneumonia
10. Suicide[34]

In a society that values preparedness, people put a priority on physical and mental health. Many of the causes of death you see above are brought about by lifestyle choices – lack of exercise, poor diet, alcohol and tobacco abuse. While it's true we all have to die of something, we can increase our productivity to society if we engage in preventative care, sensible diet and exercise. An extended emergency with limited infrastructure will require a tremendous amount from you; that's not the time to realize you are out of shape and dependent on medications to function.

And there's evidence suggesting that we're making progress in the area of house fires. According to the National Fire Protection Association (NFPA), civilian deaths from home fires have steadily declined in the last 35 years. In 1977, accidental fires caused 6,015 deaths.[35] That number has steadily dropped since then, hitting a point in 2012 with only 2,380 deaths, a sixty percent decrease.[36] If our society decided to make fire preparedness a cultural priority, we could lower that death rate further.

Then there's the protection of property. Improvements in fire safety have yielded not only reduced deaths from house fires; they've also reduced the economic burden associated with repairing or replacing the home. The NFPA estimates that fire losses cost society $5.7 billion in 2012 (in 2012 dollars). While that's a significant amount of money, it's also the least costly year for fire damage compared to the 35 years preceding it.[37] The data from NFPA makes the point we all need to hear: when we make life safety a priority, through using better building materials and safety technology, we can reduce injuries and damage to property.

Better building codes would also greatly reduce property damage from severe weather. Louisiana State University's Hurricane Center did extensive studies on the damage caused by Hurricane Katrina. The researchers reached a breathtaking conclusion: stronger building codes in Louisiana alone would have eliminated 80 percent of the wind damage caused by the storm, saving approximately $8 billion in losses.[38]

In addition to better building codes, creating a culture of preparedness would lead people to voluntarily invest in other things which would reduce property damage, such as:

- Hail resistant roofs
- Fire extinguishers

- Burglar alarms
- Landscaping designs for use in areas with high wildfire risk

Finally, there's a financial toll – one that goes beyond simply repairing damaged property - that should be included as well. Let's return to the example of fire safety and look at the CDC's data for 2010:

Fire and burn injuries represent 1% of the incidence of injuries and 2% of the total costs of injuries, or $7.5 billion each year.

- Males account for $4.8 billion (64%) of the total costs of fire/burn injuries.
- Females account for $2.7 billion (36%) of the total costs of fire/burn injuries.
- Fatal fire and burn injuries cost $3 billion, representing 2% of the total costs of all fatal injuries.
- Hospitalized fire and burn injuries total $1 billion, or 1% of the total cost of all hospitalized injuries.
- Non-hospitalized fire and burn injuries cost $3 billion, or 2% of the total cost of all non-hospitalized injuries.[39]

Most of us don't factor the medical costs into a calculation of economic damage. The data from the CDC should convince us to do otherwise. Just a 50 percent reduction in fire and burn injuries would result in a $3.75 billion savings. Might a preparedness culture help reduce these damages?

Think about the businesses affected by disasters. The Small Business Administration, relying on data from the Institute for Business and Home Safety, concluded nearly a quarter of businesses affected by a major disaster fail to re-open.[40] How much capital is lost as a result of a failure to re-open? How much business goodwill? How much life savings vanish when a business fails to reopen due to a disaster? How many jobs are lost as a result? What financial and economic distortions do disasters create in communities when businesses fail to stay afloat after a disaster? If you work for a business, how certain are you that your employer will come back on line and provide you with a job and steady pay check?

A culture of preparedness that simply inspires people to learn basic skills and make common sense preparations around their home and business can save countless lives, property and financial resources. Note that in the above examples, we did not have to buy a single firearm, water purification system or a year's worth of freeze-dried food. That's not to say that you shouldn't own these things as part of your preparedness plan; rather, being prepared means executing the basics very well. And even executing the basics can have a dramatic impact on the resiliency of our communities in an emergency.

ARE THERE ANY INDIRECT BENEFITS OR BY PRODUCTS FROM HAVING SUCH A CULTURE IN AMERICA?

In addition to the benefits discussed above, there are other benefits that, while not directly related to preparedness, certainly make us a smarter and better society. For example:

- We improve our science acumen. Learning about things like solar power, water purification, weather, first aid, gardening and ham radios help educate us how the natural world around us works.
- We reduce crime through effective self-defense training. Learning skills to avoid and handle dangerous situations improves our overall safety.
- We increase acumen in government and constitutional rights. People who engage in the preparedness culture pay attention to the issues affecting their government, taking an active role as a citizen participant in local affairs.
- We develop a sense of community when we prepare with others. As Professor Matt Davis points out, those participating in community preparedness efforts report not only a sense of psychological well-being from doing so, but also closer relationships with their neighbors.

IS THERE A CASE AGAINST CREATING A CULTURE OF PREPAREDNESS?

What might we save if we did not adopt such a culture?

We would certainly spend less money on preparedness efforts. We would not need to spend time learning skills. We would simply outsource these functions to others, such as government agencies. For example, we could task FEMA and other local emergency management agencies with all disaster recovery and preparedness. They would be responsible for feeding and caring for people after a disaster. This would certainly require taxpayers to pay more in taxes to fund such an effort. We would also need to be willing to pay more taxes to provide the additional manpower needed for police, fire and EMS.

But isn't that what we are doing now? Have we not seen enough evidence of our nation's de facto preparedness plan, which seems to involve waiting for the federal and state government to tell us what to do and to provide us with bottled water and military rations after a disaster? Don't we already rely upon FEMA debit cards and low-interest loans to rebuild?

Are you happy with the way we currently prepare and respond to disasters? If not, are we willing as a nation to do something about our lack of readiness?

WHAT ABOUT OPSEC CONCERNS?

OPSEC, or "operational security," dissuades many in the preparedness movement from sharing information or knowledge with others, lest their stored supplies be discovered and requisitioned. Before you cast aspersions on people who feel this way, consider the fact that the Federal Bureau of Investigation has deemed bulk purchases of MREs, waterproofed match containers and flashlights as a "potential indicator of terrorist activities."[41] Is it any surprise that many people prefer to keep their preparedness efforts confidential?

I certainly sympathize with those who have OPSEC concerns. I am frustrated by the fact that one federal agency (FEMA) tells us to "make a kit and have a plan," while another agency (the FBI) simultaneously asks disaster preparedness vendors to report purchases of items that would be handy to have in an emergency. Apparently, there's a certain amount of preparedness items the federal government wants us to have. What that amount is, of course, remains a mystery.

Everyone has to make their own decision as to what degree of information they share about their efforts. If you believe as I do that the movement needs more leaders, let me encourage you to focus less on the threat of marauding neighbors and invasive governments and instead focus more on the good we can do by making our communities more resilient.

Please hear me correctly: I am not saying you shouldn't protect yourself nor object to an overreaching government. Both are definitely qualities we should all have. At the same time, if society is going to benefit from a culture of preparedness, we have to be the ones to effectuate the change. And we won't be able to do that if we cloister ourselves away from others, refusing to be the change agents desperately needed.

Many people of faith are called to be those change agents. Can our faith lead us to be better prepared?

PIVOT POINTS:

- Creating a culture of preparedness is no different than creating any other type of culture in America.
- When urging people to better prepare themselves, we should be able to explain it in terms of lives saved, property protected, costs contained and communities strengthened.
- Being engaged in preparedness efforts teaches us much about things beyond preparedness – math, science, handiwork and critical thinking skills all come into play.
- We should not let our fear of people finding out we have made preparedness efforts dissuade us from becoming apostles in the movement.

ON FAITH

For me personally and for many Americans, faith guides us in all aspects of life. That means we need to understand what guidance our religious tenets provide to those of us who prepare for various perils.

As a Christian who has studied the Bible over the years, I have found a number of passages in both the Old and New Testaments directing adherents of the Abrahamic religions who seek guidance in these texts to prepare themselves for hardship. For these faiths, preparing for tough times remains mandatory to this day. I cannot speak to what other faiths provide their adherents in the way of guidance on this subject, but it's reasonable to expect other religious beliefs encourage vigilance and readiness for adversity.

I realize many may not care what the Bible says about preparedness, and my choice to address the role of faith is not part of an effort to evangelize to others. Non-believers are free to skip this chapter. However, given the central role that faith plays in the lives of many, I believe it would be negligent of me not to include this discussion. In the following pages, I will make the case that Christians have ample Biblical authority to prepare for a wide spectrum of threats that face our country. Those Christians purport to follow Scriptures containing a variety of guidance on many aspects of life, including the need to be prepared. If we are serious about building a culture of preparedness in America, we need to understand how faith can play a role in that construction.

Lest you think our government has not thought of this, consider FEMA's use of "Clergy Response Teams" to help get the word out to Christians that they are to obey the government's edicts in times of crisis.[42] These teams would use scripture – Romans 13 – to try to convince American Christians to do what their government tells them to do. While people of faith and civil liberties advocates may take issue with the government's decision to rely on pastors using Christian scripture in an effort to increase compliance with government mandates, it's clear FEMA understands that faith plays a role in preparedness and dealing with the aftermath of a disaster.

NOAH

We begin our discussion in – where else – the book of Genesis. In the sixth chapter, we learn that "Noah was a righteous man, the only blameless man living on Earth at the time. He consistently followed God's will and enjoyed a close relationship with him."[43] And for this reason, the Lord made a promise to Noah, telling him "I solemnly swear to keep you safe in the boat, with your wife and your sons and their wives."[44]

We learn a number of things in these two verses. First, Noah was a standup guy. He's the kind of person we would want as a neighbor, regardless of your religious beliefs. It's rare that the words "righteous" or "blameless" are used to describe anyone. No doubt he was a leader in his community. We also see that Noah took his leadership role within the family very seriously. Otherwise, God would not feel compelled to have protected them. By promising to protect his family, the Lord knew he could count on Noah to focus on the task at hand.

Noah was given very detailed instructions on how to build the ark. The Lord told Noah to

make a boat from resinous wood and sealing with tar, inside and out. Then construct decks and stalls throughout the interior. Make it 450 feet long, 75 feet wide, and 45 feet high. Construct an opening all way around the boat, 18 inches below the roof. Then put three decks inside the boat – bottom, middle, and upper – and put a door in the side.[45]

In addition, the Lord said

bring a pair of every kind of animal – a male and a female – into the boat with you to keep them alive during the flood. Pairs of each kind of bird and each kind of animal, large and small alike, will come to you to be kept alive. And remember, take enough food for your family and for all the animals.[46]

We learn from this text that God sweats the details so that we don't have to. The Lord knew exactly how big to make the boat, what design the use, and what materials to use. Noah was not left to his own devices to guess how to go about constructing something that would fit the job. All he had to do was trust the Lord and follow his guidance.

Finally, note that the Lord told Noah to be a prepper: his instructions included storing enough food for his family and for the animals for an extended period.

I've always thought Noah probably caught a fair amount of grief from his fellow citizens. After all, who in their right mind builds a boat the length of one and a half football fields? If that wasn't bad enough, the Lord instructed Noah to board the boat with his family and all the animals an entire week before the floods came.[47] Yet Noah stayed focused, knowing that he had been called to prepare himself, his family, and the animals for the calamity ahead.

After the flood waters receded and all of the living creatures disembarked from the ark, the Lord told Noah to "be fruitful and multiply. Fill the earth."[48] The Lord's plan for Noah and his family wasn't simply to survive the flood. He had a purpose for Noah and his family: to establish and rebuild a community, better than the one the Lord just destroyed.

What can we learn from Noah's story?

- The Bible calls Noah a righteous man. We should strive to be like him.
- When you hear the voice calling you to prepare for hard times, don't dismiss it. It could very well be from the Lord.
- Preparedness isn't about being a winner after a calamity. Preparedness is a means to an end. Here, the Lord prepared Noah and his family not

so they could be the "winners" after the disaster, but instead so they could play a role in the rebuilding process.

• When we are creating our preparedness plan and acquiring what we need, we do not need to fret over the details or the needed resources. As Abraham told Isaac on the way up the mountain where Isaac was to be sacrificed, "the Lord will provide."[49] In Isaac's case, the Lord provided an alternative sacrifice to spare his life. If the Lord is calling you to be better prepared, you can rest assured he will provide you with the means to do so.

• God made sure Noah provided for the animals. We should do the same for our pets and livestock to the best of our abilities.

JOSEPH

If there were an ultimate survivor contest in the Bible, Joseph surely would win. Sold into slavery by jealous brothers, the wife of his master falsely accused him of rape. Joseph was thrown into jail, only to be promoted to oversee everything that happened within the prison, including being in charge of all the other prisoners. Later, when he interpreted the dreams of Pharaoh, predicting seven years of bountiful harvest and seven years of famine, Pharaoh tapped Joseph to oversee a massive food storage program so that the people of Egypt would not starve.

He clearly demonstrated wisdom and God's guidance when making recommendations to Pharaoh on how to proceed:

"Therefore, Pharaoh should find an intelligent and wise man and put him in charge of the entire land of Egypt. Then Pharaoh should appoint supervisors over the land and let them collect one-fifth of all the crops during the seven good years. Have them gather all the food produced in the good years that are just ahead and bring it to Pharaoh's storehouses. Store it away, and guard it so there will be food in the cities. That way there will be enough to eat when the seven years of famine come to the land of Egypt. Otherwise this famine will destroy the land." [50]

What made Joseph so successful?

- "The Lord was with Joseph and blessed him greatly as he served at the home of his Egyptian master."[51] Despite mistreatment by his brothers, Joseph did not feel sorry for himself. Nor did he feel vengeful. He did his best under the circumstances – no matter how bad those circumstances were - working diligently for his employer.
- When Pharaoh asked Joseph to interpret a dream for him, Joseph wisely said "it is beyond my power to do this... But God will tell you what it means and will set you at ease."[52] Joseph was not looking for credit or self-promotion. He knew from whom all blessings flow.
- Joseph refused to be angry with his brothers, realizing that God used their actions to help save many lives in Egypt from starvation.[53] He did not let his circumstances define who he was and what he could accomplish.

Note Joseph's interpretation on how best to prepare for the disaster was a beautifully simplistic formula: *save a portion of your production (in our case, most likely money) and use it to acquire things you might need during the lean years. Secure and take care of those extra supplies you keep so that they will be available to you during the famine.* So many people shy away from increasing their own readiness because it's perceived as being too hard or too expensive. The scriptures tell us that if we feel called to be better prepared, we simply need to follow the examples set by Joseph and other godly people.

One last note about this story – none of this would have happened if Pharaoh lacked the foresight to follow the recommendation to be prepared. We need leaders in government who are willing to listen to wise counsel, especially the counsel of people inspired by faith.

NEHEMIAH

Nehemiah's account of the rebuilding of the walls of Jerusalem should be required reading for anyone in the construction business or for anyone seeking guidance on how to act in faith in the workplace. As his workers rebuilt the walls, Nehemiah made sure that the safety needs of his team were met:

> When our enemies heard that we knew of their plans and that God had frustrated them, we all returned to our work on the wall. But from then on, only half my men worked while the other half stood guard with spears, shields, bows and coats of mail. The officers stationed themselves behind the people of Judah who were building the wall. The common laborers carried their work with one hand supporting their load and one hand holding a weapon. All the builders had a sword belted to their side. The trumpeter stayed with me to sound the alarm.[54]

Even as we go about our daily lives, scripture tells us we should be mindful of our surroundings and equipped to deal with them. That doesn't mean we need to be fearful of everything and everyone around the corner. We should be alert and ready to protect ourselves and help others.

Nehemiah also understood that all of us have a role to play in the security of our communities. Consider his efforts to create something akin to a neighborhood watch:

> I said to them, "Do not leave the gates open during the hottest part of the day. And while the gatekeepers are still on duty, have them shut and bar the doors. Appoint the residents of Jerusalem to act as guards, everyone on a regular watch. Some will serve at their regular posts and some in front of their own homes."[55]

He appreciated the fact that able bodied citizens have a role to play in the security of our communities. Even if we're not on guard as a gatekeeper, we are called to be vigilant around our own homes.

JESUS

We read in Luke 22 some of the final instructions the Prince of Peace gave to his disciples shortly before his arrest:

> Then Jesus asked them, "When I sent you out to preach the Good News and you did not have money, a traveler's bag, or an extra pair of sandals, did you need anything?"
>
> "No," they replied.
>
> "But now," he said, "take your money and a traveler's bag. And if you don't have a sword, sell your cloak and buy one! For the time has come for this prophecy about me to be fulfilled: 'He was counted among the rebels.' Yes, everything written about me by the prophets will come true."[56]

Similarly, at another time Jesus made a whip and expressed his anger with those who defiled the temple:

> It was nearly time for the Jewish Passover celebration, so Jesus went to Jerusalem. In the Temple area he saw merchants selling cattle, sheep, and doves for sacrifices; he also saw dealers at tables exchanging foreign money. Jesus made a whip from some ropes and chased them all out of the Temple. He drove out the sheep and cattle, scattered the money changers' coins over the floor, and turned over their tables. Then, going over to the people who sold doves, he told them, "Get these things out of here. Stop turning my Father's house into a marketplace!"[57]

Here we have two examples of Jesus either arming himself or encouraging others to be armed in order to carry out a mission. The passage in Luke is perhaps the more instructive story of the two, as he clearly tells his follow-ers to arm themselves with the preferred personal protection device of that era – the sword.

Some will say the passage in Luke is simply another parable and shouldn't be taken literally. Yet closer to the time of his arrest, Jesus told his disciples that he would no longer speak to them using figures of speech, to ensure they clearly understood his instructions.[58] Further, we see an interesting shift in Jesus' com-ments between Luke 21 and 22. In chapter 21, he continues to speak in riddles and rhetorical questions, whereas in chapter 22, he speaks in quite literal terms throughout the chapter.

Jesus knew trouble would follow his team in the days ahead; as predicted, they were "counted among the rebels." He wanted them to be prepared to deal with whatever might come their way, not simply for the sake of staying alive, but to enable them to carry out the important work of spreading the message of eternal life.

Further, consider Jesus' teaching about the ten bridesmaids:

Then the Kingdom of Heaven will be like ten bridesmaids who took their lamps and went to meet the bridegroom. Five of them were fool-ish, and five were wise. The five who were foolish didn't take enough olive oil for their lamps, but the other five were wise enough to take along extra oil. When the bridegroom was delayed, they all became drowsy and fell asleep.

At midnight they were roused by the shout, "Look, the bridegroom is coming! Come out and meet him!"

All the bridesmaids got up and prepared their lamps. Then the five foolish ones asked the others, "Please give us some of your oil because our lamps are going out."

But the others replied, "We don't have enough for all of us. Go to a shop and buy some for yourselves."

But while they were gone to buy oil, the bridegroom came. Then those who were ready went in with him to the marriage feast, and the door was locked. Later, when the other five bridesmaids returned, they stood outside, calling, "Lord! Lord! Open the door for us!"

But he called back, "Believe me, I don't know you!"

So you, too, must keep watch! For you do not know the day or hour of my return.[59]

I think most of us get the sense after reading this text that it's a harsh ending. Yet when we fail to prepare for the various crises that can happen in life, a harsh outcome is often the result. Jesus isn't hoping for a bad result for anyone. He is sounding an alarm for all of us to be prepared, both spiritually and temporally.

For those of us who are interested in preparedness, what can we learn from Jesus?

We need to be good stewards.

In the Parable of the Talents, Jesus tells a story about the man who entrusted gold to his workers for safekeeping. Two of the workers invested the gold and increased the amount returned to the man. One worker did nothing productive with the gold he was given, returning the exact amount he'd been tasked with managing.[60] The man praised the two who invested the money entrusted to them. But he scolded the one who failed to demonstrate good stewardship by depositing the money so it could earn interest.

If we applied the message from this parable as to how it might apply to the Christian who is trying to decide whether to become better prepared, we might conclude that:

- God has blessed many of us with things like homes, vehicles, a job, good health and families. We are obligated to take care of those blessings.
- Our preparedness obligations require effort and cannot be ignored. Like the men who invested the talents, preparedness to protect what we have requires work on our part.
- God will provide a way for you to improve your preparedness.

Although not all of us have the same skill sets or resources, we can all do something to enhance our personal readiness.

We are to be vigilant and keep watch.

Jesus describes the end days in stark terms:

> However, no one knows the day or hour when these things will happen, not even the angels in heaven or the Son himself. Only the Father knows.
>
> When the Son of Man returns, it will be like it was in Noah's day. In those days before the flood, the people were enjoying banquets and parties and weddings right up to the time Noah entered his boat. People didn't realize what was going to happen until the flood came and swept them all away. That is the way it will be when the Son of Man comes.
>
> Two men will be working together in the field; one will be taken, the other left. Two women will be grinding flour at the mill; one will be taken, the other left.
>
> So you, too, must keep watch! For you don't know what day your Lord is coming. Understand this: If a homeowner knew exactly when a burglar was coming, he would keep watch and not permit his house to be broken into. You also must be ready all the time, for the Son of Man will come when least expected.[61]

We are called to constantly keep watch. We don't know when the Lord is returning. Nor do we know the exact date and time the next tornado will hit our community, when a tire on our car will blow out on the interstate, or when we will suffer an economic setback. By being vigilant and keeping watch, we can possibly avoid some of those perils and be prepared to deal with them if they do occur.

We are called to be ready to help meet the temporal needs of others.

Jesus said:

> For I was hungry, and you fed me. I was thirsty, and you gave me a drink. I was a stranger, and you invited me into your home. I was naked, and you gave me clothing. I was sick, and you cared for me. I was in prison, and you visited me.
>
> Then these righteous ones will reply, "Lord, when did we ever see you hungry and feed you? Or thirsty and give you something to drink? Or a stranger and show you hospitality? Or naked and give you clothing? When did we ever see you sick or in prison and visit you?"
>
> And the King will say, "I tell you the truth, when you did it to one of the least of these my brothers and sisters, you were doing it to me!"[62]

Compare that with the encouragement found later in the New Testament:

> If someone has enough money to live well and sees a brother or sister in need but shows no compassion—how can God's love be in that person?
>
> Dear children, let's not merely say that we love each other; let us show the truth by our actions.[63]

A number of people in the preparedness movement believe their only goal is to survive any scenario they might face. And while being able to endure a disaster is a goal we should all strive to achieve, simply surviving it doesn't do much to improve our communities. People of faith are called to prepare themselves so they can be ready to help others less fortunate and be leaders in the community to address the rebuilding process. For a Christian to plan otherwise is inconsistent with the teachings of the church.

Many will no doubt chafe at my suggestion that preppers ought to be prepared to help others in their time of need. After all, it's challenging enough to set aside provisions and training for ourselves and our families. Those who fail to do so should not tax those who do. Believe me; I get it. It's frustrating to hear people with nice homes, jobs, cars and penchants for nice vacations tell me "when things get bad, we're just going to head to your house."

Yet consider the urgings of James Wesley Rawles, one of the experts in the field of preparedness. He strongly advocates for those in the prepared-ness community to be prepared to be charitable during a crisis.[64] Charity to those in need is good preparedness. People whose physical needs are being met are less likely to resort to self-help in order to survive. They are stronger, healthier people, meaning they can do their part to help restore order as well.

Charity does not mean, however, that people are required to put them-selves or their families at risk by giving their entire larder away or by handing it out themselves, making them vulnerable to attack. Rawles believes there are effective strategies and policies to deal with such issues.[65] I don't believe you're required to take in every family that shows up at your doorstep. At the same time, we need to be putting those "foul weather friends" on notice that they need to get their own preparations squared away. For those of you of faith, consider your obligations to help others get better prepared as you prepare.

But if Jesus sanctioned preparedness, how do we reconcile the passage where Jesus says don't worry about tomorrow?

So don't worry about tomorrow, for tomorrow will bring its own wor-ries. Today's trouble is enough for today.[66]

I would encourage you to read the verse before that particular one – and perhaps the entire chapter in question (Matthew 6) while you have your Bible out – and put things into context. Consider the previous verse:

Seek the Kingdom of God above all else, and live righteously, and he will give you everything you need.[67]

In seeking the Kingdom of God, we are to study and act on what we learn from scripture. The scriptures make it clear – in both the Old Testament and New Testament – that we are called to be prepared to weather the storms of life, not only for our own safety but to be a blessing to others. Preparing for emergencies enables us to not worry about tomorrow, as Jesus instructed.

THE CHURCH OF JESUS CHRIST OF LATTER DAY SAINTS – WHERE PREPPING AND FAITH MERGE

If religion provides people of faith with a strong motivation for preparing, it is useful to discuss the preparedness efforts of The Church of Jesus Christ of Latter-day Saints (LDS), or as they are often called, the Mormons.

Headquartered in Salt Lake City, the Church claims 15 million members worldwide.[68] Among those members, there are 80,000 missionaries serving around the globe, which no doubt contributes to the fact the church is one of the fastest growing churches in the United States.[69]

For many Americans, what they know about the Church comes from popular culture or the Broadway show *The Book of Mormon*. Once you get beyond the common misconceptions, you learn that the Church is a very vibrant and industrious group of believers. (For the record, I have never been a member of the Church.)

Take for example their strong emphasis on emergency preparedness. Just searching the word "preparedness" on the Church's newsroom webpage reveals a number of pertinent results. In many respects, the LDS Church is the Church of Preppers. It makes no secret about its emphasis on emergency preparedness, telling families to be ready to be self-reliant in the event of a local or national crisis.[70]

The Church does not simply tell its members to prepare themselves. It actively provides specific guidance to its membership, urging them to keep food, water, cash, medication and communication plans ready in the event of an emergency.[71] This is certainly sound advice, but it begs questions: why does the Church feel it necessary to encourage its membership to be so well prepared? Why is preparedness a basic tenet of their faith?

Ezra Taft Benson, the Secretary of Agriculture under President Dwight Eisenhower and the thirteenth president of The Church of Jesus Christ of Latter-day Saints, often exhorted the faithful to be prepared, in very specific terms, calling on members to have a year's worth of supplies available to them in the event of an economic or agricultural crisis.[72] Yet Secretary Benson strongly emphasized the need to be spiritually prepared, placing that need ahead of temporal preparedness.[73]

Hearing a United States Secretary of Agriculture warn other Americans about the possibilities of economic failures, famines and other disasters reducing access to food will certainly get your attention. But note the priorities set forth by Secretary Benson: spiritual preparation followed by temporal preparation. It is evident that the Church does not advocate storing food and supplies simply to endure a disaster; they expect their members to do so in order to carry out the Church's work. Preparedness in the Mormon community is never the end goal. It's a means by which success can be achieved – being able to keep the Church going and meet its goals to help others.

WHY IS FAITH SUCH AN EFFECTIVE MOTIVATOR FOR PREPAREDNESS?

If we're going to utilize faith to encourage people to create a preparedness culture, we should understand why it works. What guidance can the Scriptures give us to shed some light on that?

The Scriptures give us advice on how to live a better life, calling us to safety. The book of Proverbs provides a wealth of guidance on how to live a healthy, fruitful life. Within Proverbs, we find a number of verses pertaining to preparedness:

3:25-26 "You need not be afraid of sudden disaster or the destruction that comes upon the wicked, for the Lord is your security."

10:25 "When the storms of life come, the wicked are whirled away, but the godly have a lasting foundation."

27:12 "A prudent person foresees danger and takes precautions. The simpleton goes blindly on and suffers the consequences."

Preparedness creates capacity to be charitable as mandated. The Scriptures call us to help others. By being able to manage ourselves after a disaster, we are in a better position to render assistance to those who, for whatever reason, need our help.

Our faith helps motivate us during those really dark times during a prolonged emergency. During a crisis, everyone seeks a source of strength. People of faith often rely on it to help energize them and stay motivated to weather the storm. As the Psalmist writes, "Even when I walk through the darkest valley, I will not be afraid, for you are close beside me. Your rod and your staff protect and comfort me."[74]

Faith can be a great tool for motivating people to take action. But how do we take an exercise of faith and turn it into a civic duty? And what about those of us who are not people of faith? Do our obligations as citizens require us to be prepared?

PIVOT POINTS:

- Scriptures used by the Abrahamic faiths provide examples, guidance and motivation to prepare for difficult times.
- Faith plays an important role in not only motivating people to prepare, but also in encouraging them to help others do the same.
- A number of churches engage in preparedness and disaster recovery efforts. For those looking to use their faith in the pursuit of preparedness, there are a number of opportunities to do so.

ON CITIZENSHIP

Good preparedness is good citizenship.
I don't think I'm advancing anything new with that proclamation. Think back to the efforts of those Americans who planted Victory Gardens during World War II. The nation's civil defense efforts during that war were largely manned by volunteers wanting to help their country. Even today, people from all walks of life respond to 911 calls as members of volunteer fire departments. These individuals demonstrate good citizenship and preparedness skills.

When communities are prepared to handle disasters, it puts less of a burden on relief agencies. That reduced burden frees those agencies to aid those who were unprepared for whatever reason. Furthermore, prepared people are in a better position to provide their neighbors with aid and other supplies, further strengthening the community.

One thing holding us back in creating a culture of preparedness is the mindset that preparedness is an individual sport. Many who engage in this project fear nefarious elements will learn of their supplies and efforts, making them a target during a disaster. Others are concerned that the government will attempt to take their supplies during a crisis, so that they can be redistributed to those who fail to prepare.

In some respects, we in the preparedness movement are our own worst enemy. While we're waiting and preparing for that worst case scenario – where society descends into full bore collapse - to tell all of our haters "tough luck," what are we going to do in the meantime? Shouldn't those with a passion and knowledge share it with others? Isn't the goal of this effort for us and our communities to survive? What's the point in individuals surviving if you're left with chaos and the collapse of services, resulting from the fact that others didn't prepare? We need a change, away from an *"I've got mine...too bad you don't have yours!"* attitude to a more patriotic tone, where we work to create a culture in which people make preparedness a priority – as in it becomes second nature to us.

I am not judging those who think that way, for I myself have been guilty of such thinking in the past. Tired of the ridicule and criticism from those who thought my need to be better prepared was a quirky hobby at best or symptom of a mental illness at worst, at times I found it hard to justify efforts to help others learn to prepare. Winning in preparedness – being able to feed, hydrate and shelter yourself during an extended emergency when others cannot – may make you feel better now. But in the long run, humans have proven to be incredibly resilient. Many who didn't prepare will not perish. They will still be our countrymen after the crisis. Preparedness puts you in a position to be a leader in that inevitable rebuilding process, during which we can improve our communities and society. And being a leader means we have to set a good example now so that people will follow our example during and after a crisis.

Look at it this way. If ninety percent of those people in the Superdome hiding from Hurricane Katrina had a good plan, some supplies, and some know how, would they have fared better? Probably so. Of course, it would have meant that government agencies, local community groups, and preparedness advocates – *that would be us* - would have gone into the community well before storm season to help folks in economically distressed areas of town start making plans and learning a few skills.

Admittedly, many in the United States have a growing skepticism about the government's ability and motives when it comes to preparing us for disaster and protecting us from terrorism. To wit:

- *The government's lackluster response to various disasters.* It's hard for the American people to take our government's readiness efforts seriously when we see how those efforts play out at disaster time. While I don't think all of the criticism leveled at the government's response to Hurricane Katrina is warranted, it's clear that there was a degree of confusion at the Federal level. Consider the explanation of then-Secretary of Homeland Security Michael Chertoff, regarding the federal response: "[We assumed that] there would be overflow from the levee, maybe a small break in the levee. *The collapse of a significant portion of the levee leading to the very fast flooding of the city was not envisioned.*"[75] (emphasis added.)

Yet such a breach had been predicted and the results of such a breach extensively analyzed by the New Orleans *Times-Picayune* and others long before Hurricane Katrina.[76]

• *Gun confiscation in the aftermath of Hurricane Katrina.* Days after Katrina came ashore, officers of the New Orleans Police Department began what is best described as door to door gun confiscation. "No one is allowed to be armed. We're going to take all the guns," New Orleans Superintendent of Police P. Edwin Compass III pronounced.[77] NOPD took approximately 700 guns from law abiding citizens by threat of force.[78]

• *Tactics associated with the acquisition of military grade hardware by state and local law enforcement.* Local law enforcement agencies continue to acquire various pieces of military hardware, such as Mine-Resistant Ambush Protected (MRAP) vehicles, through so called "1033 programs." These programs allow the military to dispose of their used or otherwise unneeded materials to local law enforcement agencies. Guns, aircraft, and armored response vehicles are just some of the gear your police department can obtain through this program.[79] The events in Ferguson, Missouri in August 2014 showcased the tremendous amount of military hardware a local police force can acquire.

While it is certainly reasonable for law enforcement agencies to be well equipped for the protection of officers and to deal with emergencies and criminals, the tactics utilized by many of these agencies, coupled with this military grade hardware, changes the nature of the relationship between law enforcement and the community. In what was previously a community-based policing effort, focusing on protecting and serving, more police departments are moving towards an aggressive "flash bang the house and shoot the family dog" approach to law enforcement.[80] Aside from the wasteful spending by the federal government which necessitates this program to unload unneeded military hardware, it helps militarize our police force and diverts resources away from programs that could be used to help prepare citizens for disaster readiness and communities for disaster response.

- *The labeling of those with certain political beliefs as possible "terrorists."* You would think we'd learned a thing or two from McCarthyism, but apparently some lessons have to be re-learned from time to time. You can imagine the ire of civil liberty groups when a report from the Missouri Information Analysis Center (MIAC) on "The Modern Militia Movement" described a number of groups as potential domestic terrorists. According to the government's report, possible terrorists included people who:
  - oppose strict gun control
  - are bearish on the U.S. economy
  - oppose the North American Union
  - oppose a federal income tax
  - oppose illegal immigration
  - oppose the Federal Reserve
  - display political material from the Constitutional Party, the Libertarian Party, or campaign materials from such candidates as Ron Paul.[81]

Less than a month after the report was issued, the director of the Missouri Department of Public Safety apologized to the political candidates named in the report – Ron Paul, Bob Barr and Chuck Baldwin. In his apology letter, the director stated "it is the judgment of the Department of Public Safety that the report should have made no reference to supporters of [2008 Republican Presidential candidate] Ron Paul, [Libertarian Party Presidential nominee of 2008] Bob Barr, [Constitution Party Presidential nominee of 2008] Chuck Baldwin or of any other third-party political organization or candidate."[82]

Such a finding from a government agency is likely little comfort to those who fear a government's preparedness effort. At times, the government's preparedness efforts appear light on meaningful readiness and heavy on the infringement of citizen rights and liberties.

When such stories are reported by the media, it's no surprise the typical American who wants to be better prepared has reason to lose confidence in the government's ability to deal with crises. When stories about the government purchasing over one billion rounds of hollow point ammunition – despite the fact that even conservative websites like Breitbart.com conclusively proved that such purchases were not as breathtaking as originally reported[83] – it predictably fuels concerns over the government's ability to not only keep us safe but its willingness to infringe upon the liberties of its citizens under the guise of protecting us.[84]

Despite these concerns, we in the preparedness movement need to set aside our fears of marauding criminals and door to door MRE confiscation by the government and start actively encouraging others, if not outright helping them, improve their level of readiness. Many within the preparedness movement are quick to chastise the "sheeple" - a pejorative term comparing those outside the movement to animals with a strong herd mentality, like sheep. Despite being critical of those people, precious few of these critics engage in any activities which would help educate and prepare their fellow citizens for disaster.

Building a culture of preparedness means entire communities are part of the culture. And if you are an advocate of preparedness, I would argue that it is your patriotic duty to help other citizens do the same. Note I'm not suggesting that you go out and buy emergency kits for all of your neighbors, although that would certainly be a nice gesture. It does require that you be available to provide guidance and suggestions to them, along with encouragement. It means being generous with your time, and perhaps even your finances, in helping others get prepared for a disaster.

As vanguards of the preparedness movement, not only do we need to be demonstrating good preparedness; we need to be demonstrating *good citizenship*. These two concepts are inseparable. Consider the following from the U.S.

Seventh Circuit Court of Appeals in the landmark case of *Welsh v. Boy Scouts of America:*

> A great deal is at stake in the interpretation of statutes such as Title II. The Founding Fathers recognized that a republic cannot endure without a virtuous citizenry. **Successful self-government requires that citizens willingly participate in public affairs, make sacrifices for the common good, curb their selfishness, and join in taking responsibility for themselves and others.** The central question for those concerned about maintaining the health of our republic must be, "how do individuals acquire the virtues necessary for self-government?" History provides only one answer: through the institutions of civil society, like the family, religious groups, and voluntary associations, which inculcate a sense of moral values in the young. Throughout its eighty-six years of existence, **the Boy Scouts have successfully presented its combination of educational, social, athletic, craft, wilderness training and outdoor activities to our young people**.......When the government, in this instance through the courts, seeks to regulate the membership of an organization like the Boy Scouts in a way that scuttles its founding principles, we run the risk of undermining one of **the seedbeds of virtue that cultivate the sorts of citizens our nation so desperately needs.**[85]

(emphasis added)

Some will disagree with the court's ruling in the *Welsh* case, which permitted the Boy Scouts of America to require its membership to affirm a belief in God. Yet I don't think anyone can seriously argue that the justices of the U.S. Seventh Circuit Court of Appeals were incorrect in holding that "successful self-government requires citizens...tak[e] responsibility for themselves and others." The Boy Scouts of America – and other organizations like them – encourages its members to participate in public affairs and take responsibility for their readiness not as a means to promote their own fortunes, but as a way to improve self-government and encourage good citizenship.

Being an advocate for preparedness means being a model citizen. In an effort to create aspirations for those of us in the movement wishing to improve their citizenship skills, I've identified thirty precepts to hopefully guide us towards becoming better members of our communities and in turn better advocates for preparedness.

1. *You are responsible for your own safety, well-being and happiness.* Although there are others who may be in a position to help, it's not the government's job, church's job, nor the family's job to provide for a healthy adult's well-being. You are ultimately responsible for your situation. We are all born with some sort of gifts as well as limitations. What we do with them is up to us. The attitude we choose towards life is just that – our choice. Those whose preparedness plan is nothing more than following the instructions of government officials, depending on them for food, water and shelter will be sorely disappointed in the quality of their lives post disaster. Just ask those in New Orleans after Hurricane Katrina.

2. *Followers are a dime a dozen. We need leaders.* People associate being a leader with holding some sort of elected office in government, the local PTA or HOA board. But we can all be leaders without ever holding office. Leaders are the ones who demonstrate good citizenship, a willingness to work hard to help the community, exhibit wise thinking and knowledge, and inspire others to do the same. Don't be afraid to do these things. We have plenty of couch sitters in society. We need more people out doing – leading a scout troop, teaching a Sunday school class, picking up litter on the side of the road, teaching others important skills, and sharing what they know with others. Our nation is short of leaders offering preparedness solutions. If you want to see more people being self-reliant, lead your own effort to make it happen by first being a leader in your community.

3. *Help others, even when it's sometimes inconvenient to do so.* Be charitable. Tithe to your local house of worship or charities of your choice. Offer to help your friends when they need something. Help them when they move into a new home or need a ride to the airport. Have them over for dinner. Serve on the board of a non-profit organization or other civic group. When you help others, you demonstrate you are concerned with their well-being by making an investment of your time and attention in them. This makes you more effective when you encourage them to prepare.

4. *Build relationships.* Write notes to people to let them know you're thinking about them. Reach out to those who are ill. People listen to whom they trust and value. By building relationships, we put ourselves in a position to effectively encourage people to be more prepared for emergencies.

5. *For those who have done a lot for you, do a lot for them.* Some people are givers by nature. If someone has done a lot to help you or your kids, do the same for them to the extent you can. Don't be a taker. Acknowledge their contributions to you by going the extra mile for them. Effective preparedness requires a sense of community. The givers are the people you want on your team.

6. *When you commit to doing something, see it through.* Your friends and neighbors need to know that when you say you will do something, they can take it to the bank. If you say you'll man the grill for the neighborhood barbeque, do it. When you say you'll provide beverages and snacks for the school's fundraiser, do it. The world is full of people who agree to do things and then flake out. Don't be a flake. You are a survivor. Survivors are not flakes.

7. *Never stop seeking the truth.* As Samuel Arbesman pointed out in his book we previously discussed, much of what we think we know is wrong. Information and innovation change the way we think about and do things. Never be satisfied that you know enough about the economy, politics, science, or God. Never assume all of your opinions are correct. Have

enough character to be willing to re-examine what you know to ensure you are on the right track. In a grid down situation, you will need every ounce of your analytical abilities and knowledge. Don't shortchange yourself by failing to grow mentally.

8. *Never stop self-improvement.* Work incessantly on physical fitness, spiritual development, the impression you make, and your attitude towards life and others. People who do so are seen as leaders. Operating under emergency conditions will require you to function at peak performance in every aspect of your life. Condition yourself now for that contingency.

9. *Be in the know.* Know what the weather forecast is. Know what's happening in the financial markets. Know what political issues are front and center at all levels of government. Know what radio stations carry news, weather and traffic bulletins. You may get little warning before an emergency. Not being completely clueless as to what's going on around you will help you prepare.

10. *Toughen up.* Being prepared for an emergency requires a tremendous amount of mental, physical and emotional toughness. It's not the time to be weak. Learn to do difficult things without complaining. Things are not nearly as bad as you often think they are. Nor are they as bad as they could be.

11. *Get a gun and know how to use it safely and effectively.* The gun is one of the greatest life safety tools ever invented. It can give an 80 year old woman a fighting chance against a 25 year old attacker. Seek out a good instructor who can help you learn. Effective and safe gun ownership isn't hard to learn, but it does take a commitment to do so. Guns are an important part of our nation's history. You keep the tradition alive when you learn to shoot safely and effectively.

12. *Be able to provide for your family's needs in a grid down environment for at least 90 days.* Originally when I wrote this, I felt you should be able to provide for your family for an entire year. However, I'm a realist — most people will do well to be self-sufficient for 90 days. If you can manage

on your own for three months, you can weather all but the most cata-strophic emergencies. This will put you in a position to help others in a crisis.

13. *Be happy in your own skin.* So many today live through the lives of others, enabled by the growth of reality television. If you're constantly improv-ing yourself, you are making the best with what you have. Be happy with that. Don't fret over what you don't have. It won't do any good. It will also condition you to not fixate on what you're lacking during a protracted emergency.

14. *If you are a person of faith, be active in your local house of worship.* This may not sound like an obligation of citizenship. I can assure you people of faith are in need of good examples of other people of faith being active in their community. By being active in your church as well as your community, you get the benefits of spiritual guidance in your own life, the lessons of which you can apply to your civic work as well. And if you are not a person of faith, consider becoming active in a secular civic organization.

15. *Be a good steward of what you have.* This includes not only your finances but also your home, your body, your tools, and the environment. Make the stuff you own last. Ensure that what you have is reliable and in good working order. The power outage affecting your neighborhood is not the time to realize your generator isn't working due to neglect. Eat healthy. Get regular check-ups.

16. *Read good books.* Reading fiction from time to time can be stimulating, but books on politics, the economy, history and how to do things on your own offer practical knowledge that can be useful in surviving a disaster.

17. *Learn new skills that would be beneficial in a crisis.* Welding, first aid, solar electricity, gardening, wood working, making repairs around the house, firefighting, ham radio, and preparing food in a grid down environment would all be helpful skills to have. If you can do some of these things well, your help will be in high demand in an extended crisis.

18. *Be a model citizen.* Vote. Be courteous in public. Hold doors open for people. Offer to help someone reach an item on the top shelf at the grocery store. Don't be a jerk. Don't litter. Don't do anything you don't want caught on surveillance camera and shown on the local news. Respect the rights of others, even if you don't agree with their cause. Look for ways to help people. When you see large objects lying on the freeway, call 911 and asked them to send someone out to remove them to help avoid accidents. Pick up nails and screws you see lying in the roadway or parking lot to help you and others avoid getting a flat tire. Return stray grocery carts in the shopping center parking lot back to where they belong. Your 30 seconds of assistance to someone may help them in some fashion that's worth far more than 30 seconds of your time. In addition, others may see you and emulate your example.

19. *Share your knowledge with others and encourage them to prepare.* There are countless ways to do this. My wife and I once had our supper club group over with a disaster food preparation theme – we demonstrated a variety of storable foods and alternative cooking methods to our friends. Forward articles to them on various threats we face and ask "What's your take on this? Do you think this is something we should be prepared for?" Let them know that while you'll do what you can to help them during an emergency, you won't be able to provide for all of their needs in a crisis. They will need to be prepared to take care of themselves.

20. *Never stop instilling positive thoughts and ideas into your kids.* This may seem like an unusual precept for a book about disaster preparedness. But your kids need to understand they are special, strong, and capable of handling any challenge thrown at them. Note I am not saying you should coddle your kids, turning them into mush. They need to understand hard work and failure. They also need to understand that you love them regardless and that you think they can thrive during life's challenges. Set a good example for them. When you make a mistake, own up to it. They need good examples of how to handle failure and mistakes, too.

21. *Never forget the sacrifices of those before you.* A tremendous number of Americans have given their lives so that we could be free. Our ancestors have worked hard and lived earnestly in order to put you and me into a better position than they were in. For example, my parents were rather poor when my father was in dental school. My mom made his lunch for him daily, and to save money, she packed his sandwich in an old bread wrapper she re-used every day for that purpose. Years later, when I heard that story, I began packing my own lunch sandwich in an old bread wrapper, as a daily reminder to me to be thankful and appreciative of the sacrifices my parents made to give me the opportunities I have today.

22. *Confront evil.* Note I did not say "confront evil with extreme violence." We must confront evil in order to eradicate it. Confronting it means dealing with evil in a purposeful manner. Bring it to people's attention. Take action to the extent you legally and morally can to end it.

23. *Find what motivates you and use that to your advantage.* We are all motivated to prepare for different reasons. Some of us relish the opportunity to challenge ourselves in a grid down environment. Others are motivated to prepare to protect their families. Many prepare because they want to help others in the community. Find what motivates you – even if it's fear of a zombie apocalypse – and use that as your motivation to push your preparedness efforts.

24. *Show no favoritism towards the poor or the wealthy.* Class warfare has permeated all aspects of our political debate. It's unbiblical to favor one group over another based on their financial status. We're told in the book of James that we should not favor the rich over the poor.[86] Similarly, we're told in Leviticus not to favor the poor over the rich.[87] We require federal judges to take an oath stating they will "do equal right to the poor and to the rich."[88] If you're guilty of this, stop it. In a crisis, the poor person who has handy-man skills becomes rich. The wealthy person you detest may have resources you may need to survive. These two individuals may need each other in that situation.

25. *Pay attention to your surroundings.* Where is the nearest exit? Can you describe the suspicious person you see in the neighborhood? What is the license plate number of his or her vehicle? Does that parent with two little kids at the grocery store need your assistance? Good citizens are attentive to the world around them.

26. *Make an everyday carry (EDC) kit.* You can take a small flashlight, a pocket knife, a section of paracord, and a cell phone almost anywhere in America. Learn new ways to use these items effectively in an emergency. Never leave the house without them. Have it nearby wherever you are. Most of us will never have to fight our way through the chaos spawned by a crazed gunman at the mall or live through a protracted economic collapse. The odds are much higher that you will need to illuminate a darkened parking lot or cut a length of string to tie something together. Good citizens prepare themselves to handle large and small emergencies.

27. *Choose your close friends well.* Earlier I mentioned the need to build relationships with a variety of people; that suggestion still stands. When it comes to choosing your close friends, choose well. Choose people who value good citizenship like you do. They don't have to be preppers, but they do need to share your core values. They need to be people who are givers like you. They need to be solid, reliable, stand-up kind of people. Don't look for people your own age, profession, religion, sexual orientation, nationality or race. Things like that don't matter when the flag goes up. You need to know they pack the gear – mentally, physically, and emotionally – to help out in times of trouble.

28. *Know what you will do in the event of a fire, severe weather event, emergency medical event, or threat of violence.* Learn how to do CPR and use a fire extinguisher. Get a weather radio and use it. Think about what you'd do if there were an act of violence in the various places you visit daily.

29. *Patriotism is citizenship in action.*[89] Consider the efforts of FreedomWorks, a libertarian leaning change agent in American politics. Regardless of whether you agree with their goals, I think their Rules for Patriots is

required reading for anyone interested in moving the needle on any political or social cause. One of their best pieces of advice – for which I can vouch from my own professional experience – is that those who are taking action often get the results they want.[90] Those who go to their government representatives or community leaders and promote change are the ones who get heard. Those who stay home and hope the nebulous "they" do something about it will have no say in what the final product looks like. Your neighborhood isn't likely to get serious about preparedness unless you start the conversation. Your house of worship isn't likely to encourage its members to take steps to be more self-sufficient unless you urge the organization's leaders to take an interest in doing so.

30. *When you travel, have a set of emergency supplies that stay in your suitcase.* Some emergency foods, a small AM/FM radio, some first aid items, a few extra batteries for your flashlight and radio can come in very handy during an emergency when on the road.

Many of these precepts may not sound like guidance on improving the quality of your citizenship. But as Dr. Richard Lee and Jack Countryman noted in their book, *God's Promises For The American Patriot,* patriotism is simply citizenship in action.[91] There are things we need to be doing not just because it's good preparedness, but because it's good citizenship. It's good citizenship to be able to take care of ourselves and help others in need during a time of crisis. By doing so, we reduce the burden placed on government and other aid agencies in time of a crisis, freeing them up to help others.

Our journey towards better citizenship may take us in many different directions. In determining how we're better able to be the solution rather than part of the problem, we need a basic understanding on a macro scale what the solution looks like. The search for this macro analysis takes us into the hearts of some of the greatest think tanks in the United States, where erudite scholars pour over data and concoct new ideas on how best to solve the problems created by our lack of preparedness.

Welcome to the study of Preparedness Public Policy.

PIVOT POINTS:

- Good preparedness is good citizenship. We have an obligation as citizens to strengthen our nation by being a resilient people.
- Being a good citizen means setting a good example. By doing so, you gain the respect of others and can be an influence in their lives when it comes to encouraging them to prepare.
- Live by a code – a clear set of values and beliefs which exhort you to help others, be earnest in your work and commitments, and make sacrifices if needed.

PREPAREDNESS
PUBLIC POLICY

I majored in Public Policy Studies in college. At my alma mater, the typical major required about 30 semester hours of course work in a particular discipline. Majoring in Public Policy Studies, on the other hand, required 56 semester hours in several disciplines, nearly half the hours required to graduate. Those of us who elected to major in it were gluttons for punishment.

Does public policy play a role in creating a culture of preparedness? Policymakers in Washington and in various state capitals have been trying to use the disciplines of political science and economics to shape the preparedness landscape for quite some time. Does that mean the government should be setting policies to encourage preparedness? Or is that better left for individuals to do for themselves, free from government interference (or subsidy)?

The use of hurricane preparedness tax free holidays serves as a prime example. Currently, four states – Alabama, Louisiana, Texas and Virginia – have sales tax-free holidays limited to various preparedness supplies. The big winners are the citizens of Louisiana: not only do they not pay sales tax on the first $1,500 of sales price of a plethora of preparedness items (including flashlights, radios, plastic sheeting, fuel tanks, batteries, portable generators, and nonelectric food storage coolers), they have a separate sales tax holiday weekend applicable to the purchase of guns, ammunition and hunting supplies.[92]

The thinking behind such programs goes something like this: if we reduce the price of preparedness supplies, more people will purchase them, thus reducing the number of people needing assistance after a disaster. Corporations

wanting to sell supplies will use their own marketing dollars to encourage people to stock up on needed disaster items. It's Economics 101: reduce the price of
preparedness goods, and more people will purchase them, holding other things
constant. Makes sense, right?

Researchers at The Tax Foundation take issue with that. Studying the various
state tax holidays across the country, the organization concluded such holidays
do not lead to people buying more preparedness items. It contends consumers
simply wait to buy things they were already planning to purchase during tax free
weekends.[93] Further, research indicates many retailers raise prices during sales
tax holidays, reducing the actual benefit consumers expect to receive during
sales tax-free shopping.[94]

The Foundation singled out Virginia's hurricane preparedness sales tax holiday for further analysis. Virginia exempts a number of helpful items during
its sales tax holiday, such as cell phone chargers and duct tape. Yet other similar items, such as laptop chargers and electrical tape are not exempted. The
Foundation goes on to point out that if these items are such good preparedness
purchases, shouldn't they be exempt year round? In the end, the organization
concludes sales tax holidays are less about good preparedness and more about
making those politicians who support sales tax holidays look good.[95]

Regardless of whether preparedness sales tax holidays are sound policy or
political gimmicks, the fact state legislators and governors are even willing to
consider them as a means to help create a culture of preparedness is a good sign.
While the Tax Foundation makes salient points about the effectiveness of such
strategies, I don't want to criticize those policymakers who are trying something
new in order to get people better prepared.

Addressing the public policy issues surrounding preparedness in one chapter is challenging. Policy wonks have written extensively on the proper role of
government in responding to and preparing for disasters, seeking to find that
sweet spot in the nation's public policy that will yield the best results in the most
cost efficient manner.

Some of the most helpful analysis on the subject of disaster public policy
comes from the Foundation for Teaching Economics ("FTE"), a 501(c)(3) organization dedicated to teaching young people how to apply economic thinking to

public policy issues, as well as to help teachers become more effective at teaching critical economic topics.[96] Their study entitled "Economics of Disasters" represents a significant drill down into the issue of how governments and communities typically respond to disasters from a public policy perspective. It's difficult to do justice to their efforts with only a few bullet points, which is why I highly recommend you read their work on this subject yourself if you find this particular topic meaningful to you.

On the issue of the government's role in the post-disaster environment, the FTE believes there are three important roles for the government to play:

1. Determine when the government should take an active approach versus allowing other, more qualified institutions to take the lead on certain recovery tasks.
2. Establish and enforce the rule of law, both from a civil and criminal perspective.
3. Provide the public goods – such as infrastructure and first responders – critical to recovery.[97]

As you might imagine, the FTE takes a skeptical view of the government's ability to be all things to all people in the post-disaster environment, noting that government intervention often leads to unintended consequences. Even though such programs may be well intentioned doesn't mean they are sound public policy.[98]

What strategies, then, do public policy experts prefer? While this is not meant to be an exhaustive list (since not all experts agree on the solutions), it will help you get a sense for some of the more common approaches suggested by the policy wonks on how to make America better prepared for disasters.

Mandatory Building Codes

Many may think "mandatory building codes" is a redundant phrase; after all, isn't a building code "mandatory" if it exists?

It turns out you can have building codes without necessarily making them mandatory. Here in Texas, a natural disaster-prone state that touts its pro-business philosophy towards regulations, the state legislature adopted the International Residence Code (IRC) as its state building code. Read the language in the Texas Local Government Code carefully:

Sec. 214.212 **INTERNATIONAL RESIDENTIAL CODE**. (a) To protect the public health, safety, and welfare, the International Residential Code, as it existed on May 1, 2001, is adopted as a municipal residential building code in this state.

> (b) The International Residential Code applies to all construction, alteration, remodeling, enlargement, and repair of residential structures in a municipality.
>
> (c) A municipality may establish procedures:
>
> (1) to adopt local amendments to the International Residential Code; and
>
> (2) for the administration and enforcement of the International Residential Code.

Sounds rather authoritative, right? Yet notice the language in subsection (a), where it says the IRC "is adopted as *a* municipal residential building code in this state." The word "a" means it could be one of a number of options a city could follow. (Replacing the word "a" with the word "the" would be a good start on fixing this problem.)

Further, notice the text in subsection (c) where it says "a municipality *may* establish procedures…for the administration and enforcement of the International Residential Code." There's some wiggle room in there; the "may" means a municipality could elect not to adopt any procedure to administer or enforce the building code.

The Insurance Institute for Business and Home Safety (IBHS) summarized the Texas building code situation like this:

Texas does not require mandatory adoption and enforcement of its residential building code throughout the state. However, municipalities may adopt and enforce the 2006 IRC as a minimum residential construction code. The Texas Department of Insurance has adopted windstorm building code standards, but they are voluntary requirements that homeowners must meet for the purpose of obtaining windstorm and hail insurance from the Texas Windstorm Insurance Association (TWIA), the state wind catastrophe pool.

* * *

Adoption of a modern statewide code system throughout the state would help establish uniformity in enforcement and application of the code provisions, and reduce losses in the event of catastrophic events.[99]

In the 18 most hurricane prone states, IBHS ranks Texas —with its 367 miles of Gulf of Mexico coastline - fifteenth in adequacy of building codes and enforcement. This is despite the fact Texas has adopted the IRC as a statewide building code.[100]

If the public policy fairies could sweep down to the Lone Star State and sprinkle building code dust from El Paso to Texarkana, what changes in the building codes might ensue?

First, the IRC (or similar standard) would become the mandatory building code for all of Texas, both in the cities as well as the unincorporated areas of the state. Those municipalities and counties lacking the funding for enforcement and administration would either need to raise the money locally - most likely through building permit fees - or the state would have to provide it for them.

Second, the building codes would need to specify special standards for those who live in disaster prone areas, like near the Gulf coast. (The IRC already has model language that, if adopted, would make homes more disaster resistant.) In addition, the IBHS would recommend all of the various contractors who build homes be licensed and obtain regular continuing education.[101]

So why don't governments enact mandatory have building codes or meaningful licensing requirements for those in the construction trades? Aside from the cost of enforcement which would be borne by the local and state governments required to enforce them, many complain that they add to the cost of the home. These additional costs, the argument goes, cause consumers to do one of three things:

- Buy a smaller home with fewer features;
- Buy a home with the safety upgrades required by code, leaving less money for improvements such as upgraded counter tops, swimming pools, and media rooms; or
- Buy a home in another part of the county or state that has less restrictive codes and enforcement.

None of these choices are particularly appealing to many buyers. Yet when we are contemplating the cost to society of having a large number of homes lacking basic storm resistance features in a storm prone area, we might want to reshape the argument away from "strong building codes keep buyers from getting granite countertops and nice patios" to "building codes keep your kids from getting sucked out of your home when the tornado or hurricane hits your community."

Building codes represent best practices in building with an eye towards life safety. They reduce damage from both a human as well as a financial standpoint.

REFORMS TO DISASTER MITIGATION FUNDING

No discussion on the public policy of preparedness would be complete without discussing federal aid money. And that brings us to Robert Stafford.

Robert Theodore Stafford served as a U.S. Senator from Vermont for eighteen years, having also served in the U.S. House of Representatives, and as attorney general, lieutenant governor and governor of Vermont. Perhaps known best for the Robert T. Stafford Student Loan Program named after him, his influence on legislation went far beyond higher education.

In 1988, the Robert T. Stafford Disaster Relief and Emergency Assistance Act amended the Disaster Relief Act of 1974.[102] While the act has been amended since, the fundamental purposes of the law remain intact: encouraging the development of disaster plans and providing federal assistance programs after disasters.[103]

Stafford Act grants for mitigation efforts – those designed to *prevent* damage – yield tremendous savings. According to a study done by the Multihazard Mitigation Council on the efficacy of federal dollars spent on mitigation, FEMA mitigation grants have produced an overall benefit-cost ratio of four to one. That means for every dollar of mitigation expense, four dollars are saved in the form of reduced storm damage. Further, the Council measured tax dollars that would have been spent on things like disaster recovery and future hazard mitigation but were saved because of these mitigation grants. It found a 3.65 to one ratio of savings for every dollar of federal funds spent. In short, mitigation efforts pay for themselves in reduced damage costs and reduced disaster recovery expenditures at nearly an eight to one return.[104]

In light of this data, a number of interest groups have urged Congress to pass the Safe Building Code Incentive Act.[105] This legislation would change the Stafford Act funding formula for states affected by a disaster. Those states that enact and enforce a statewide building code would receive an additional four percent of federal funds after a disaster compared to those states that do not. This would incentivize states to step up their efforts to enact and enforce damage-reducing building codes in order to avail themselves of additional funds at disaster time.[106]

DISASTER SAVINGS ACCOUNTS

Earlier, we discussed the decision by states to have sales tax holidays to encourage preparedness purchases. Not to be outdone, some in Congress have their own version of a tax saving plan to stimulate preparedness.[107]

Similar to health savings accounts (HSAs), a disaster savings account (DSA) would permit taxpayers to exempt up to $5,000 of income from federal income taxes.[108] Money put into a DSA could only be used for certain preparedness expenditures, such as safe rooms, flood prevention and reinforcing structures for earthquake risks.[109]

The DSA concept seems to assuage some of the concerns stemming from sales tax holiday plans. Unlike sales tax free weekends for preparedness items, DSA funds can be spent at any time of the year and on a wider array of readiness expenses. Further, the money such accounts would free up for preparedness expenditures could be far more significant than the sales tax savings that citizens would otherwise see.

As evidenced above, mitigation efforts pay for themselves in reduced expenditures for repairs after a disaster. Those reduced expenditures mean homeowners spend less money and live in safer homes as a result.

PAINTING OURSELVES INTO A CORNER

In detailing these various proposals, we inadvertently stumble upon an anomaly in thinking within many parts of the preparedness movement. Many preppers profess to hold libertarian ideals, preferring the government not venture into regulating safety (like mandatory building codes) or disaster relief funding. Can preppers be of a libertarian mindset while advocating for the changes I describe above?

In an earlier chapter, I mentioned Samuel Arbesman's theory that much of what we think we know is incorrect. We often make assumptions that a particular group of people holds a certain set of beliefs, when in fact that may not be the case. The Libertarian Party (and in the interest of full disclosure, I am a card carrying member) does not formally oppose building codes in its platform.[110] It does oppose certain codes to the extent they inhibit or restrict people from entering professions or starting their own businesses.[111] A number of state Libertarian Party organizations have been more specific, however, in calling for the end of building codes.

Ideological purity with any political party's position is rarely a barrier to entry, although the Libertarian Party and its affiliate state parties often require its candidates have a high degree of congruency with the official party platform.[112] I'm not convinced that a libertarian leaning prepper must disavow any beliefs in the benefits of building codes or federal disaster assistance in order to make a meaningful contribution to the cause of liberty and smaller government. If we accept the notion that people will expect the government to provide disaster relief as a political reality, then what is the libertarian response to that? Some might argue that the best approach, assuming that political reality is true, is to take steps to ensure that those who benefit the most from disaster aid undertake mitigation efforts to help reduce the need for tax dollars going to them after a disaster. Put another way, homeowners need to have more skin in the game if they expect the government to provide them with federal aid after a disaster. Enhanced building codes are one way we can make that a reality.

In the end, politicians, regulators and policy advisors will continue to use public policy tools at their disposal to advance various agendas and ideals. Fortunately, there are a number of tools available which would reduce the financial impact of disasters while increasing the readiness for disasters and resiliency after them. It takes political courage to undertake many of these efforts. Policymakers must be willing to set aside partisanship, emotions and even good intentions and instead look at data and facts in order to formulate the best approach to advancing a preparedness culture in America.

How do you and I encourage our leaders to do so? *By encouraging them to stand up for sound public policy that promotes preparedness.* When we build relationships with our local and federal legislators and regulators, we are in a better position to encourage them to take up meaningful legislation and policies, like better building codes and incentives to invest in mitigation efforts. Many will shun the idea of building such relationships with our government leaders, claiming it's too difficult, too time consuming or just futile. Yet that's precisely what those who have been successful in changing government policies over the years have done. We need to be doing what those successful advocates in the past have done for their issues of interest.

As is often in the study of public policy, we learn that many political and policy issues have their own third rail so to speak. What is the third rail of preparedness?

PIVOT POINTS:

- Successful preparedness advocates have a basic understanding of the public policy issues pertaining to an improved national resilience and readiness.
- Policy makers have a number of tools and options at their disposal. We need to encourage them to use those tools in a way that promote resilience and save tax dollars. These issues necessarily touch on political positions and realities.
- Successful advocates will be able to transcend party affiliations and encourage leaders from all parts of the political spectrum to find a political pivot point to support preparedness policies, consistent with the leaders' own political positions.
- We need to engage our government leaders and build relationships with them as a way to improve preparedness public policy.

THE THIRD RAIL

S omewhere in the annals of preparedness literature, there is a set of rules which apply to all writings on the subject. One of those rules is crystal clear: *in any comprehensive book or manual about preparedness, you must talk about the need to be armed.*

Guns and weapons are the third rail of preparedness. In some circles, religion is the proverbial third rail – meaning the subject we don't touch because it's fatal to civil discourse, much like touching the third rail of a subway track would expose you to extremely high voltage. In discussing meaningful fiscal reforms within our federal government, some politicians and policymakers refer to Social Security as the third rail. Many subjects worth discussing have their own third rail; ours is just as polarizing as any other.

I debated whether to even cover this subject. I decided to include it so as to equip gun owning preppers on some best practices and messaging when discussing gun ownership in the preparedness context. I also wanted to share some food for thought with non-gun owning preppers as well.

I don't want my discussion or my beliefs on the issue to discourage anyone from engaging in the effort to create a culture of preparedness. Admittedly, I am taking some risk here by bringing this up. But I have faith that those of you who are truly interested in helping to create the culture will hear me out, form your own opinion, and still be willing to engage in the effort regardless of your position on guns.

Can someone be a part of preparedness culture if they choose not to have a firearm? We are called to be prepared by FEMA, our religious tenets, and various civic organizations; how someone chooses to go about doing that is their business. Many in the movement opt not to have weapons. While I think such a strategy is incomplete, I don't think less of those who make that decision. We have liberties in how we go about enacting our preparedness obligations. Our job is to be supportive of other preppers, teaching to and learning from each other. If our biggest debate in the preparedness movement is whether we should be armed, it will be a signal to all of us that we've made major strides in the level of national readiness.

Why do citizens need guns anyway? How do weapons build up the culture of preparedness, especially if their ownership and use are controversial to some? I can think of three reasons why those who want to be prepared for a wide spectrum of perils would want to have a reliable firearm as one of their preparedness tools.

FIRST, POLICE CANNOT BE EVERYWHERE, ALL THE TIME.

When people need to defend themselves, they need to do it immediately. Waiting for law enforcement to arrive isn't an option, even in areas where police response times are excellent. BusinessWeek concluded that using the government's own data, one can conservatively assume that Americans use guns 100,000 times a year in legitimate DGU – defensive gun use. BusinessWeek then concedes that the actual number could be far greater than 100,000 times a year – perhaps as much as 370,000 times a year.[113] Sticking with the conservative number, we can determine that citizens use guns to defend themselves and families 274 times a day.[114] On the high end, that daily number skyrockets to 1,013 a day – some 42 times an hour.[115]

In a crisis, police response times increase dramatically, to the point where citizens are often required to fend for themselves. During the Los Angeles riots in 1992 and the Ferguson, Missouri riots in 2014, many business owners armed themselves to protect their livelihoods and lives from the senseless violence. And the peril in the post-crisis environment need not be rioting. National Public Radio reported in 2006 that violent crime in New Orleans increased dramatically a year after Hurricane Katrina hit the city.[116]

A prepared family living in an area affected by such an emergency will have the means to protect themselves from harm. Police, Fire and EMS services cannot be everywhere, all the time.

SECONDLY, GUNS EMPOWER CITIZENS IN THE EVENT OF WAR, TERRORISM OR CATASTROPHIC FAILURE OF GOVERNMENT.

The Oath of Allegiance, required by every person wishing to become a citizen of the United States, *in toto:*

> I hereby declare, on oath, that I absolutely and entirely renounce and abjure all allegiance and fidelity to any foreign prince, potentate, state, or sovereignty, of whom or which I have heretofore been a subject or citizen; that I will support and defend the Constitution and laws of the United States of America against all enemies, foreign and domestic; that I will bear true faith and allegiance to the same; that I will bear arms on behalf of the United States when required by the law; that I will perform noncombatant service in the Armed Forces of the United States when required by the law; that I will perform work of national importance under civilian direction when required by the law; and that I take this obligation freely, without any mental reservation or purpose of evasion; so help me God.[117]

In addition to new citizens, we also require members of Congress[118] and the military[119] to take similarly worded oaths.

Earlier in the book, we talked about preparedness being an obligation of good citizenship. I cite this oath as further evidence of that proposition. After all, to be able to meet these obligations, we need to be prepared and equipped to do so.

Note the language in the oath with regards to enemies "both foreign and domestic." The concept of a foreign enemy doesn't tax our imagination. We can think of other nations who might plot to attack the United States.

Defining the "domestic" enemy, on the other hand, may raise a number of questions by well-meaning citizens. Who might be a domestic enemy? Presumably, a domestic enemy would be one attempting to overthrow a duly elected constitutional government or engaging in terroristic acts against the American people. In a worst case scenario, it might include defending the rule of law and human life from marauders during periods of a catastrophic failure of government institutions.

Anyone interested in what modern-day devolution of government and economy might look like should read *This Was Not Our War — Bosnian Women Reclaiming The Peace* by Swanee Hunt.[120] As the U.S. ambassador to Austria from 1993 to 1997, Ambassador Hunt spent many hours interviewing women who were victims of the conflict in Bosnia. These women – professional, vibrant, some of whom were educated in the United States – tell hellish accounts of the atrocities committed during the conflict.

What struck me was how quickly people in Bosnia — even those with means - became refugees in their own country. These successful, educated women struggled to wrap their minds around what was happening as the violence escalated. Many endured extreme conditions, including deaths and assaults of close family members, hunger, and lack of medicine and sanitation. As I read their heartbreaking accounts, I kept wondering if their situation would have been different had their families been armed and prepared to deal with a crisis. After all, only 50 years had passed since the end of World War II; the memories of that war were still in the collective memory of many of the region's residents.

It's important to remember that this part of the world wasn't a third world hotspot. Sarajevo hosted the 1984 Winter Olympics; just seven years later, conflict in the region broke out, culminating into the largest humanitarian disaster in Europe since World War II.

Americans often think things like the Bosnian conflict happen to "those people over there" and cannot happen here in the United States. We had similar thoughts about terrorism prior to September 11. Let me be clear: I think it's safe to assume the odds of such atrocities happening here under our constitution and republican form of government are small. But should we simply rely on such assumptions, never allowing ourselves to contemplate or prepare for the unthinkable? Or should we heed the advice of the former secretary general of Interpol — the international police organization — and encourage an armed citizenry to deal with significant dangers from foreign and domestic enemies?[121]

This notion of an armed citizenry protecting its individual liberties and lives did not evolve over the last twenty years. Consider the writings of the abolitionist Frederick Douglass. A former slave who escaped bondage to become a prolific orator and writer on the subjects of freedom and liberty, Douglass had what would no doubt be a controversial view today about gun ownership:

> From the first I saw no chance of bettering the condition of the freedman until he should cease to be merely a freedman and should become a citizen. I insisted that there was no safety for him or for anybody else in America outside the American government; that to guard, protect, and maintain his liberty the freedman should have the ballot; **that the liberties of the American people were dependent upon the ballot-box, the jury-box, and the cartridge-box; that without these no class of people could live and flourish in this country.**[122]

(emphasis added)

In case you were wondering, the cartridge-box to which he referred is a box of ammunition. As Douglass pointed out, good preparedness is good citizenship. Good citizenship requires we be prepared to carry out those obligations concomitant with it.

FINALLY, WHEN FACED WITH AN EXTENDED EMERGENCY, WE MAY HAVE TO HUNT AND GATHER FOR OUR OWN FOOD.

I doubt few will argue with me on this point. Heaven forbid we experience an emergency of such a scale where we're required to hunt for our next meal. If that were the case, we would want the ability to have the right tool for the job. Preppers need the ability to find a meal and acquire it when the odds are against them.

HOW SHOULD PREPPERS APPROACH THOSE OPPOSED TO GUNS ABOUT BECOMING BETTER PREPARED?

For preppers who are strong supporters of the Second Amendment, we need to make sure we do not inadvertently dissuade someone from joining our preparedness efforts because they disagree with us on the need for an armed citizenry. We need those who may not share our position on firearm ownership to join our efforts to build a culture of readiness; we cannot afford to alienate them.

Remember that everyone has a different pivot point that will cause them to plot a course towards better readiness. Your pivot point will likely be different than theirs. As long as we are getting to the same destination – a better prepared community, ready to meet a variety of perils – it's not that important as to how we get there or why we're motivated to do so.

It's time we focus on the last of the three central questions I pose: how do we go about building a culture of preparedness?

PIVOT POINTS:

- Firearms can be a controversial stumbling block in the effort to create a culture of preparedness. We need to be able to make the case for why they are necessary.
- At the same time, we should recognize not everyone will agree with the notion that preparedness requires being armed. Gun rights advocates who want to see more Americans get better prepared should not discourage people from preparing simply because they disagree on this issue. Instead, those on both sides of the gun issue should identify

common goals in the effort to create the preparedness culture and work together to accomplish those.

- Our nation's history is intertwined with the history of gun evolution and technology. Learning to use a firearm is not only a good safety skill to master; it also enables one to participate in a national tradition.

HOW

Most Americans love American culture. There may be some aspects of it we don't like (certain reality TV shows and the proliferations of gossip magazines come to mind), but offered an opportunity to trade the American experience for that of any other nation, most of us would take a pass. Our culture is vibrant, diverse and dynamic. It reflects the needs and wants of our fellow citizens on a macro scale.

That's not always a good thing, as there have been parts of our culture that have not been desirable. One hundred fifty years ago, it was both legal and culturally acceptable in parts of the United States to own fellow human beings. It's only been sixty years since Rosa Parks refused to give up her bus seat.

But as in the examples above, and countless others, the dynamic nature of American culture means we remain capable of changing it in a more positive direction. Many would agree that the culture change towards recycling waste materials and consuming more organic foods reflect positive steps for our nation. These two culture shifts did not stem from some random force of cultural physics, understood by only a handful of Ph.Ds in college campus laboratories. Cultural shifts have been taking place in our country precisely because the laws of cultural physics can be appreciated – and utilized – by anyone.

If cultural phenomena in America can be changed, is it worth the time and effort to create a culture of preparedness? Note I'm not pitching a new idea here. Quite to the contrary: in the last decade or so, a number of authors and government agencies have tried to tackle this very issue.

In 2006, the Bush administration issued a report entitled "The Federal Response to Hurricane Katrina: Lessons Learned." In the report, the administration laid out its vision for a culture of preparedness:

> The second element of our continuing transformation for homeland security perhaps will be the most profound and enduring—the creation of a Culture of Preparedness. A new preparedness culture must emphasize that the entire Nation—Federal, State, and local governments; the private sector; communities; and individual citizens—shares common goals and responsibilities for homeland security. In other words, our homeland security is built upon a foundation of partnerships. And these partnerships must include shared understanding of at least four concepts:
>
> - The certainty of future catastrophes;
> - The importance of initiative;
> - The roles of citizens and other homeland security stakeholders in preparedness; and
> - The roles of each level of government and the private sector in creating a prepared nation.[123]

One of the more well-known proponents of creating such a culture is retired Army Lt. General Russel Honoré. You may know him best from his role in helping manage the emergency in New Orleans after Hurricane Katrina. With his book, *Survival — How Being Prepared Can Keep You And Your Family Safe,* General Honoré started his own initiative to create a culture of preparedness.[124] Speaking at the 2009 Homeland Security S&T Stakeholders Conference, General Honoré shared a story about a conversation with a cousin, in which his cousin complained to him about the government's response to their community after Hurricane Gustav. After they walked the affected property together, General Honore' noted his cousin's boat and football tailgating equipment. He concluded by telling his cousin that if he took storm season as seriously as hunting or football season, he wouldn't need as much help from the government.[125]

The Obama Administration noted the need to educate our youth on creating a culture of preparedness – a time-tested practice in changing American culture. From the Obama White House website:

> Every year the disasters we see are different but the educational programming we provide in schools, home, and churches is constant. The American Red Cross in partnership with the Serve Illinois Commission supports AmeriCorps members in their work to educate thousands of pre-kindergarten through 12th graders how to make a life-changing difference in an emergency. To date our youth preparedness program has engaged over 400 AmeriCorps members and triple that in volunteers. I talk about creating a culture of preparedness; I see it in the AmeriCorps serving, and those that have served, and I see it daily in the kids learning from them.[126]

Irrespective of what you might think of the political positions of Presidents Bush and Obama, it's clear from the efforts of their administrations that both Team Red and Team Blue appreciate the need to create a culture of preparedness, calling on individuals to take responsibility for their own readiness.

HOW DO WE DEVELOP A CULTURE OF PREPAREDNESS IN AMERICA?

If we are to create a better prepared citizenry, we must learn to speak the language of a wider audience. We must find the pivot points of our friends and neighbors to encourage them to become better prepared. We must be prepared to show them simple, cost-effective ways to quickly reach a basic level of preparedness. We must find a way to make prepping seem less of a manifestation of a mental illness and more of an obligation of good citizenship.

We must use every tool at our disposal. For parents, we must draw upon those parental instincts as a way to motivate mothers and fathers to provide for their children for an extended period of time. That means for the business person, we need to put preparedness in terms of an investment. For the investor, it means expecting companies to be prepared to carry out their day to day business in the face of weather or the normal types of emergencies. For the person of faith, we should point out the accounts in Scripture where God's people prepared for various calamities. For those active in their communities, we must demonstrate how being personally prepared will enable them to better serve the community during and after an emergency. For those citizens who believe the government will take care of them and their families in a post disaster environment, we should be able to remind them of the government's inability to take care of people after Hurricane Katrina. And if the threat *du jour* fails to come to fruition in a timely fashion, we must be ready to continue to motivate not only our friends, but ourselves, to stay prepared for a wide spectrum of possible threats to our well-being.

ARE THERE ANY EXAMPLES OF RECENT AMERICAN HISTORY THAT MIGHT GIVE US GUIDANCE ON HOW TO CHANGE THE CULTURE?

One of the best shortcuts available to us in the effort to change the culture is to learn the lessons of previous cultural change efforts. Over the last few decades, we've seen a:

- Continued decrease in the smoking rate;[127]
- Sustained reduction in the teen pregnancy rate;[128]
- Heightened awareness in recycling and environmental efforts;[129]
- Dramatic drop in the rate of bullying.[130]

As you might suspect, many of these efforts put a strong emphasis on inculcating their agenda in the minds of the young. That's because some of these issues (like teen pregnancy) are youth issues. It's also because it's easier to make a lasting change by educating the malleable mind.

Those who successfully change culture are good at setting expectations of behavior as well. For instance, health experts say that one cause of the decrease in smoking rates across the U.S. is the number of smoke-free workplaces and smoking cessation classes offered at work.[131] Employers who make cessation a priority get the result they seek. Likewise, anti-bullying advocates report that setting behavior expectations helps students understand there are consequences – both negative and positive – to their actions. [132]

Similar to these examples of successful cultural change, businesses and schools can support a culture of preparedness by providing free training and resources. If students, employees, and members of an organization believe they are expected to have an emergency kit in their car and know how to perform CPR, they will rise to the expectation, especially if there are consequences for failing to meet those expectations. Organizations that provide such training and resources are rewarded for their efforts by having employees and students who can return to work or school more promptly after an emergency.

The town of Denmark, South Carolina took a multi-faceted approach in its efforts to curb the teen pregnancy rate. Recognizing the important role of faith and churches in the community, school leaders teaching sex education courses stressed abstinence as an effective method of reducing teen pregnancy, drawing upon the prevailing religious norms in the area. By using a common message from a central faith, sex ed teachers found a familiar message that students had heard before and that parents could stress again at home. In addition, the teachers set up a mentoring program and enlisted the help of the local business community to provide free condoms. While some will undoubtedly object to some of the approaches utilized by the community, the end result is clear. Denmark went from having one of the highest teen pregnancy rates in the state to one of the lowest.[133] What can we learn from their success? Identifying and using the local community's existing resources – like institutions of faith and good corporate citizens - to reinforce the importance of the desired behaviors can lead to a change of culture.

Successful efforts were local in nature. Adam Rome wrote *The Genius of Earth Day: How a 1970 Teach-in Unexpectedly Made the First Green Generation* to explain the success of the early movement.[134] In describing Rome's premise, the New Yorker summarized the first Earth Day as locally controlled and educational in nature, as opposed to later Earth Day observations which tended to be larger and more centrally defined.[135] Earth Day 1970 focused not on creating a database of willing volunteers but rather a means to help people take action as they saw fit.[136] For our culture creating purposes, we need to emphasize local action, like the residents in San Francisco's Resilient Cities project mentioned earlier.

HOW DO WE SELL A CULTURE OF PREPAREDNESS TO A SKEPTICAL OR APATHETIC PUBLIC?

In encouraging people to "buy in" to any change in philosophy or commitment of time and resources, those of us promoting the need for such a culture should articulate why we're better off as a nation for doing so. In short, we have to have a sales pitch.

Years ago, I sold real estate as a hobby. (Yes, I have a penchant for odd hobbies.) Despite the fact I didn't do it for long, I managed to make a little money part time. But the value of what I learned from those experiences far exceeded the commissions I made. Having never sold anything in my life, I had no idea how someone goes about becoming effective at sales. Fortunately, my broker offered a number of classes and provided free audio CDs to help the newer agents learn how to sell.

Perhaps the greatest lesson I learned about selling from my real estate experience – and in my experience as a courtroom lawyer – dealt with learning to anticipate and respond effectively to objections. When we are trying to change the culture, sell a product or service to a potential customer, or get our small kids to eat their peas, we can be much more effective if we anticipate objections to our effort and have an objective, stimulating response to them.

I'll give you an example for my real estate experience. One strategy realtors and other salespeople often utilize in convincing someone to be willing to spend a little more money on a nicer home or car is to calculate what the additional per day cost is for owning the higher quality product. Let's say there's a prospective purchaser who is looking to buy a house with a price ceiling of $200,000. The real estate agent will often calculate the monthly payments for such a home. When the agent finds a home that is slightly above that $200,000 limit but has some very nice features, the agent will run the numbers again, this time calculating what the additional mortgage cost will be on a daily basis.

The pitch to spend the additional money then goes something like this:

You've told me that you don't want to spend more than $200,000 on a home, and I can appreciate that. You want to make a sound investment and manage your finances well. I think I should bring this house to your attention, however. This home we are looking at today is a bit more than your price limit, but in doing the math, I determined that for only an extra three dollars per day to your mortgage, you can have a home that has this great public school/swimming pool/ view/workshop/three-car garage (or whatever selling point the agent is trying to promote.)

Let's do some quick math based on that scenario. Over the course of a standard 30 year mortgage, an extra three dollars per day in mortgage payments would result in an additional $32,850 in payments over the life of the loan.[137] If the agent tells the prospective purchaser that it is going to cost that much to have the nicer features, the purchaser might balk at that, especially if he or she is being asked to exceed their price limit.

On the other hand, when the agent adjusts the purchaser's perspective – "for the price of a daily cup of coffee at a nice bistro, you can have this awesome media room for your family to enjoy for years to come" – it enables the prospective purchaser to rationalize the additional expense. Being able to anticipate the prospective purchaser's objection – the additional cost above their previously stated price limit – allows the salesperson to have a response which enables the purchaser to rationalize spending more than they previously planned.

Some may see such strategies as shady or underhanded. Yet the salesperson is not hiding anything or making any misrepresentations; they are simply providing the prospective purchaser with an alternative way of justifying the additional expense. In other words, the salesperson anticipated the objection (the additional expense) and provided an objective, honest, and thoughtful response to it.

We need to think like salespeople. To successfully sell others on the idea of getting prepared, it's imperative we change their perspective – by helping them mentally pivot away from focusing on the required time and expense. The successful preparedness advocate will be able to convince others to pivot their focus towards making preparedness a priority. Selling a culture of preparedness to a skeptical or apathetic public, in my opinion, requires two things:

1. An ability to effectively and quickly articulate why preparedness needs to become a priority in our communities.
2. A willingness to be personally invested in the effort.

If we are willing to develop a short sales pitch (and actually, you don't have to develop it – later on the chapter, I will give you several choose from) and be willing to make this a community service project of your own, we can develop a culture of preparedness in America that is unparalleled.

That's it.

This isn't rocket science. People have been changing the culture in this country with music, art and Bible verses for decades. There's no reason we cannot do the same. And the news gets better: there's no organization out there to my knowledge that's going to oppose our efforts. I don't see an anti-preparedness movement rising up, thwarting our attempts to get kids to learn CPR and parents to have food set aside in case of emergencies.

SO WHAT CAN YOU DO?

No doubt some of you are thinking, "What can I, just one person, do to create a culture of preparedness in my community?" A lot, actually.

I want to share some ideas which I've found to be effective at creating a culture of preparedness with my friends, co-workers, and others. Every one of you is capable of doing these things. You may come up with ideas that are far better than mine. I think you will find that in opening the discussion, you will find you have a number of people in your sphere of influence who want to be better prepared, and who just need to see someone else – someone they already trust– who is already doing it to motivate them.

What are some things you can do to start doing – right away – to build a culture of preparedness in your community?

- *Set a good example.* I put this one first since it is the public's repeated exposure to prepared people that will really move people to get prepared themselves. This not only incentivizes you to be prepared at all times, but it also helps puts the argument for preparedness in the mouth of a trusted neighbor and colleague. I am thoroughly convinced there are many Americans hungering for leadership and encouragement from average people to get better prepared; they simply need to see someone they know and like to validate their desire to improve their readiness.

  What does it mean to set a good example? It means being prepared every day for whatever may happen. You have a first aid kit at work, along with a weather radio. Your vehicles get regular routine maintenance. You have a flashlight and pocket knife with you wherever you go. You look for exits when you're out in public. You pay attention to your surroundings. You exercise those tenets of good citizenship discussed earlier.

- *Take classes to help you get better prepared and invite others to join you.* How often do your friends announce on social media they are undertaking a new hobby or training for some athletic event? If you are taking a class on CPR or gardening, why not tell others and ask if anyone would like to join you? (Don't worry if they don't...there are a lot of reasons why they might not...and not every idea is a winner). Even if you don't have any takers, you are setting an example.

- *Take active role in work place safety and security.* This could potentially be one of the most important things you do to develop a culture of preparedness. I don't think I am being overly dramatic when I say participating in your employer's workplace safety and security programs may enable you to protect countless lives.

  Depending on the size of your employer, their workplace safety program may be well-established or nonexistent. And when I say "workplace safety" I'm not only referring to perils that might cause typical workers compensation claims, but also to more serious threats, like fire, severe weather, active shooter situations or pandemics. Many times, employers are more than happy to have people take interest in workplace safety issues. Your willingness to volunteer and actively participate will likely enable you to have more responsibility – and thus more of a say – in how your company prepares for various disasters.

If you work for a large company, start by asking your human resources or facilities personnel about the existence of workplace safety programs involving employees. If one exists, get involved and participate with fervor. If it doesn't, or if your company doesn't even have a human resources or facilities department, you may be in a position to start workplace safety program on your own.

Don't know how to start such a program? Don't worry; go online and start using your search engine of choice to research articles. I would suggest that you look at the excellent resources created by FEMA on preparing your business for disaster.[138] Get your employees on a regular schedule for severe weather and fire drills. Talk to your employer about having an instructor come to work one day and teach a CPR class. Discuss with your employer's leadership team what you might do in the event that there is an active shooter on premises. Does anyone in your workplace have a weather radio in good working order? If a disaster affects your physical workplace, where are employees supposed to report the next day? There are tremendous and free resources available online from FEMA.[139]   Other online resources will enable you to get your workplace better prepared quickly and cost-effectively.

It's like we discussed before: preparedness programs go to those who show up to do the work.

- *Set up lunch and learns at work.* A few years ago, I worked in the legal department of a large insurance company. On a quarterly basis, we would have "lunch and learns" whereby we would all bring our lunch and discuss a preparedness topic. Sometimes we would watch a video on preparedness and discuss if afterwards, while other times we would bring pieces of gear for show and tell.

Word spread of our lunches, and at times we had a capacity crowd in our conference room. Such events were great opportunities for those new to the idea of preparedness to ask questions and discuss topics of interest to them. These events cost nothing and encouraged others to improve their own level of preparedness.

- *Offer to let friends and neighbors taste test your grid-down cooking efforts.* People, especially kids, like trying foods that were cooked outside on a grill, camping stove or solar oven. This is a great way to show them how easy it can be. And if you think disaster dining means you will be eating NASA-invented space food paired with canned beans, I highly recommend you pick up a copy of *The Storm Gourmet — A Guide to Creating Extraordinary Meals Without Electricity,* written by Daphne Nikolopoulos. The editor of *Palm Beach Illustrated*, Nikolopoulos demonstrates how to easily make gourmet meals with un-refrigerated foods that will impress the most discerning foodie in your group of friends. My wife, an excellent cook with a sophisticated palate, really enjoys these recipes. (I am blessed with a simple palate, allowing me to tolerate diets of pasta and cheap spaghetti sauce indefinitely.)

- *Rather than ostracizing those who don't prepare, encourage them to do so.* Many people in the preparedness movement are quick to criticize their friends, family and neighbors who don't make efforts to prepare for emergencies. We don't need critics. We need apostles. We need people in the movement to make preparedness not only attainable and prudent, but also be the "in" thing.

- *Give books on preparedness to people who show interest or to those with whom you want to build relationships.* I do this fairly often. A friend will come to me and want to talk about preparedness. If they show a strong interest in improving their readiness, I will usually send them two books. *How to Survive the End of the World as We Know It: Tactics, Techniques, and Technologies for Uncertain Times* by James Wesley Rawles and *Ragnar's Urban Survival: A Hard-Times Guide to Staying Alive in the City* by Ragnar Benson are two great books to help people jump start their efforts. Don't let the scary sounding titles put you off: these books contain valuable and practical preparedness strategies.

People are genuinely touched by gifts of books. It shows a level of interest in their lives that other people won't exhibit. By making an investment in their efforts, you are making an investment in them. That will increase your influence in their lives.

- *Set up conferences and seminars.* I've done several of these, and I find it a great way to meet like-minded people and learn some new skills my-self. "But I don't know how to go about doing something like that!" you might say. Do you think I knew how to set up a conference before I did it? I didn't have a clue how to do it. I just found a conference room to rent, partnered with a friend who runs a gun range and has a large email distribution list for marketing purposes, recruited some speakers (many of whom were my friends who had specialized knowledge in prepper topics), and went forward. If a country kid from Bell Buckle, Tennessee can figure out how to do it, I'm sure you can, too.

What should we do about the critics and the chronically skeptical? What if we're criticized and ridiculed for promoting the readiness culture? How do we deal with those individuals? Let me give you a couple of things to keep in mind.

First, for those who are Christians, remember what Jesus said in Matthew 10:14 – "If any household or town refuses to welcome you or listen to your mes-sage, shake its dust from your feet as you leave." That's good advice – don't take it personally. If you are encouraging people to ensure they can safely endure an extended emergency, you are doing a good thing. You are doing nothing for which you should be ridiculed. And I can assure you – the people who are your biggest critics will likely be the first people at your door during an emergency, asking for your help.

Second, leave the door open for them to discuss the issue with you in the future. I can tell you from personal experience a number of friends who thought my preparedness efforts were fanciful or simply the result of an overactive imag-ination have since come to me and asked for guidance on how to get better prepared. I think their willingness to come to me later on is the direct result of my willingness to leave the door open for further discussions. Changing the culture won't happen overnight, and it's unreasonable for us to think our friends will get on board with us right away.

SO WHAT ABOUT THOSE SALES PITCHES?

I'm going to give you some of my more common message points that I use to encourage people to prepare. You may come up with some that are even better. The most effective ones are the ones that come from your heart and are not something that they are likely to hear.

Here are some of my favorites:

- For me to be proven right, I only have to have one bad day between now and the end of my life to prove that my preparedness efforts were worth it. A bad storm, a serious injury, an extended power outage, or series of wildfires in the neighborhood – if I am prepared for these contingencies and need the fruits of my efforts just once, all of my efforts will have paid for themselves. In order for the unprepared person to be proven right, they have to be lucky and avoid every possible emergency, every single day, for the rest of their lives. All it takes is one incident in your life to justify your preparedness efforts.

- My wife and I regularly pay insurance premiums for our various policies. It's highly unlikely our house will burn down or that we will be in a serious automobile accident. Yet we dutifully pay these premiums – as you do – on a regular basis. While we do not expect to avail ourselves of the benefits available to us under these policies, we keep them in force because it is prudent to do so. Having said that, we are far more likely to need to know first aid or to have to deal with a power outage that we are to deal with a home destroyed by fire. If we are taking steps to manage the unlikely risk of a house fire (i.e. buying insurance for our home), shouldn't we also take steps to manage the far more likely risks such as injuries and power outages?

- "Going over to Paul's house when things get bad" is not a disaster plan. I know that sounds convenient for you, but my family has spent time and money to take care of ourselves. If you are physically and financially able to undertake your own preparedness efforts, why should you rely upon me to do it for you? Why should I pay for your refusal to prepare if you have the ability to do it for yourself?

- How convinced are you that the government can take care of you after disaster? Think about the major disasters we've had in America over the last fifteen years. Think about the response recovery efforts to those disasters. Are you comfortable placing your well-being in the hands of government agencies and charitable organizations? Even when those organizations perform well, it can still be an unpleasant experience.

- What does a year's worth of food with a long shelf life cost? It certainly depends on the types of food you buy and how many family members you'll have to feed. Bulk staples like beans, wheat, pasta, along with canned soups, meats, and vegetables can be purchased at various discount club stores and preparedness stores.

   But think about it another way – what does a year's worth of cable TV cost? A year's worth of cell phone plans for the family? A year's worth of nonsensical services many of us have on autopay on our credit cards right now that we never use? A year's worth of beer? Wine? Tobacco? Junk food?

   I'm not saying don't enjoy life. I am saying that in order to acquire the things your family needs to be better prepared for an extended emergency, it will cost some money. Don't let the expense of the niceties in life prevent you from being better prepared to endure the hardships.

- (For people of faith) What do your scriptures say about the need to prepare? Why do you think this is in the scriptures? What message is the higher being that you worship trying to tell you when the scriptures tell you about being prepared spiritually and temporally?

- If you are civic minded and active in various charities, how will you be able to really help those in need if you aren't able to feed or care for yourself in a crisis? During periods of emergencies, the need for volunteers is never higher. If you're sidelined because you don't have food, water, medicine and other necessities to take care of yourself, will you be able to be an asset to the charities of your choice, helping them out with 100 percent of your effort?

- (For parents with non-adult children at home) How much baby proofing did you do for your kids when they were little? Did you have good, reliable car seats? Did you feed them healthy foods? What steps have you taken to ensure they have what they need during an emergency? Can they escape from their room during a fire if you cannot get to them? Can you feed them for a period of time if you're not able to get food at the local grocery store? Why spend all of that money to protect them from so many hazards and yet have no plans or resources to protect them from other dangers? As a real life example, when my parents were building the home where my brother and I were raised, my mother insisted on floor to ceiling windows in our bedrooms so that we could easily get out of the house if it ever caught on fire.

WHAT ABOUT THOSE WHO CANNOT PREPARE?

In putting this book together, something began to nag at me. If we are serious about building a readiness culture, we need to address how to do so across various socio-economic lines. It's easy for those of us with a well-paying job and understanding family members to improve our readiness for various emergencies. But what about those who lack the financial or other resources necessary to prepare?

Consider just a couple of the challenges these Americans face:

Low income areas are disproportionately affected by disasters.

The Manpower Development Corporation (MDC), a North Carolina advocacy group, researched the impact disasters have on low income areas. MDC concluded those in lower socio-economic strata live in areas more susceptible to natural disasters. Lacking the financial resources to prepare, they often cannot protect their belongings or even evacuate during critical times. Once the emergency blows over, their lack of funds prohibits them from recovering the way those who have insurance and other assets do.[140]

Residents in mobile homes are more likely to be killed in tornadoes than occupants of traditional housing.

The National Severe Storm Center determined people sheltering in mobile homes or manufactured housing are as much as 20 times more likely to die from tornadoes than those residents of conventional housing. Over a recent five year period, 31% of those who died as a result of a tornado were either living in or fleeing from a mobile home, despite the fact only 8% of homes in the United States are mobile homes or manufactured housing.[141]

How do we effectively encourage less fortunate people to prepare? For folks who rely on assistance from other people and the government on a regular basis, we can:

- Focus the work of food banks to be better prepared to meet the needs of their clients after a disaster. For example, the Capital Area Food Bank of Texas – located in Austin – partners with a number of agencies and organizations to provide emergency food supplies to those impacted by disasters, as well as guidance for their clients on how to better prepare themselves for the risk of such perils.[142]
- Secure low cost training in CPR and first aid to local community groups.
- Make "community preparedness" an extension of "community policing" by having first responders help train locals on how to have an emergency plan and prepare for the possibility of evacuation.

"That all sounds great," you might be thinking. *"But who is going to pay for it?"*

These efforts could certainly be financed in part by tax dollars as part of a state or local government's public safety efforts. In addition, local civic organizations may want to help sponsor such initiatives as well. Yet those funds may not be sufficient.

Remember when I said earlier that we have to be willing to be personally invested to build this culture? We must have a willingness to put our money where our mouths are. You and I – individually, and through our churches and civic organizations - must be willing to be charitable with our time and our money to help develop this culture. I'm not saying we have to finance every effort out of our own pockets. But there may come a time where those who can afford to finance a preparedness outreach project to help youth or economically challenged communities will need to step up and do so.

Let me tell you from personal experience, it's a very rewarding way to be charitable. To see kids get trained in first aid and crisis leadership – to have new life skills enabling them to help themselves and others – because of your contribution is a very fulfilling experience.

Many in the preparedness movement see themselves as patriots. For those of us who see preparedness as an obligation of patriotism, we need to ask ourselves whether we are willing to pledge "our lives, our fortunes and our sacred honor" as our forefathers did in the Declaration of Independence to build our country. If we think of ourselves as patriots, shouldn't we be willing to make this same pledge? By accepting this pledge as our own, we should be willing to spend some of our time and resources helping strengthen our nation. That includes doing our patriotic duty to help others get prepared. Can you make that commitment? Will you make that commitment?

Who are these people who will make such a strong commitment of their time and finances to the community to help develop a culture of preparedness? I call them the Champions of Change.

Pivot Points:

- One of the easiest ways to determine how to create a culture is to study examples of where culture have been created or changed in the past. We can learn the lessons of their success.
- There are a number of things we can do to stimulate a preparedness culture. We're only limited by our imagination. If you think you lack resources to carry out your preparedness service project, partner with others who can help you. If every prepper had a service project to get others involved in the movement, think how much more resilient our communities would be.
- Those who think of themselves as patriots should consider what that term meant to the Founding Fathers and citizens whose sacrifices founded our country. We need to be willing to use our resources to improve our nation, just as they did over 230 years ago.

CHAMPIONS OF CHANGE

Creating a culture of preparedness in America will only work if the Champions of Change get into the game and make it happen.

Let's go back in history for a moment:

- The first march from Selma, Alabama during the Civil Rights movement only involved about 600 demonstrators.[143]
- Earth Day – which many credit with launching the modern day recycling movement – began as collective idea of only three people: a U.S Senator, a U.S. Congressman and an activist serving as a national coordinator.[144]
- The AIDS awareness organization ACT UP began when one person - playwright Larry Kramer- asked the question, "Do we want to start a new organization devoted solely to political action?"[145]

I've given you three examples where a small number of people started culturally shifting movements in the United States. These individuals are what I call the "Champions of Change." They were not content to simply say "something must be done to change America." They took action and inspired others to do the same. They did not back down after failures or in the face of adversity, choosing instead to pivot in a direction different from their previous efforts and work towards their goal to change America's attitudes. They continue to affect cultural change efforts.

Think about these three movements in American history. All of them, to varying degrees, drew a fair amount of criticism and opposition as they began and matured. Segregationists in the South, critics of the Earth Day movement and those opposed to dedicating resources to find a cure for AIDS mobilized their own efforts in opposition. In the case of the civil rights movement, people even lost their lives as a result of these cultural changes.

We can learn something from the efforts of these change agents. Their successes provide us with a blueprint of how to replicate that success for our own cause. And since we should not expect the same level of opposition in our efforts to change culture that those pushing for civil rights, environmentalism and AIDS awareness faced, our task should be easier than theirs.

How do we go about finding our champions? First, consider who might be interested in preparedness:

- *Active duty military and veterans.* Given the training they have received and the typical soldier or sailor's commitment to public service, these individuals often make good advocates for preparedness.
- *Law enforcement officers and other first responders.* Like those in the military, this group contains a large number of people who have important skills and a community service mindset.
- *Preppers themselves.* We are looking for those with not only a passion for preparedness but also a desire to help others.
- *Scout leaders.* Those who work with our nation's youth to train them in preparedness skills, life skills, leadership and citizenship are ideal change agents. They are already accustomed to changing the cultures and worldviews of the scouts entrusted to their leadership.
- *Boy Scouts and Girl Scouts working on merit badges.* In every community, there are young people looking for public service projects to help them fulfill merit badge requirements. As scouting encourages preparedness, getting these kids conscripted into the effort to create the culture should not be that difficult.
- *Agricultural clubs - such as 4-H and Future Farmers of America - working on safety and outdoor projects.* I spent much of my youth engaged in 4-H club

activities. These organizations have a number of programs that promote preparedness, safety and self-reliance.
- *Outdoor enthusiasts.* Many of these individuals are already into preparedness whether or not they know it. Those who spend time outdoors hiking, hunting, fishing or camping or already accustomed to thinking ahead and acquiring the skills necessary to thrive in austere conditions.
- *Sustainable lifestyle advocates.* Those who support sustainable agriculture and energy programs by engaging in backyard gardening, solar energy projects and rain water collection are prime candidates for advocating a preparedness lifestyle.

How do you find these people? Perhaps the best way is to simply start asking around. If you sat down with a sheet of paper and a pen, you could list a number of friends and acquaintances who fall into at least one of these categories. From that list, you can identify those you feel most likely would be receptive to the message of becoming an advocate for preparedness. If you meet someone in one of these groups, ask them things like:

- *Given your background, are you doing any work in personal preparedness for things like disasters?*
- *I'm looking to network with other people who are getting involved in preparedness. Do you have any suggestions?*
- *I'm working with my kid's school to help them get better prepared for the possibility of disasters. Do you know anyone who might be able to help with that effort?*

They may give you some leads...or they may tell you they are interested in the subject as well. Make sure you get their contact information and follow up with them. Not all of your contacts will pan out to be folks who you can work with to develop the culture, but some of them likely will be.

But I suspect the best source for Champions of Change are the people reading this book. If the movement is going to be successful, we need people like you – people interested in the subject and who are willing to take action.

Before you claim you lack the knowledge or experience to be an agent of change, let me assure you it is well within your skill set. I'm going to give you some detailed action steps to guide you. But remember this fundamental tenet: change does not go to the most talented. It goes to those who show up and simply do the work.

Let me share a story with you when I was able to effect change. I attended a small high school in Tennessee. The school, on its own initiative, decided to purchase an emergency siren to warn students and the community of not only severe weather but also of the threat of an active shooter on campus. When I heard the news, I contacted the school with a rather unusual request: I wanted to purchase the naming rights to the siren. After all, the school named buildings, the gymnasium and football field after people; surely the naming rights to the siren were also on the auction block as well.

With a couple of emails and a phone conversation, I became the proud sponsor of the Webb School Emergency Siren. That created an opportunity for me to get the school to consider creating a student responder program to teach students how to be their own first responders and take action in case of an emergency on campus. I helped arrange instructors to come on campus to teach students crisis leadership, tactical first aid, and communication skills with first responders. Today, student leaders receive this training at the beginning of every school year.

Before we get into the details of how to go about being the champion of change for preparedness, let me suggest something to you that will not only help you in taking on this task but in your everyday life as well. Remember this: *the process goes much easier when you have already built relationships with key decision makers.* Call it networking, schmoozing, greasing the skids – whatever you want – building meaningful, mutually beneficial relationships is absolutely essential to getting things done in a group environment. There are a number of fantastic books out there that will give you meaningful guidance on how to do this. My personal favorite is *Never Eat Alone* by Keith Ferrazzi, which I highly recommend to anyone looking for guidance on how to build professional relationships. Don't believe that good networkers are simply born with the skill set. I am living proof that you can learn how to do it.

In laying the groundwork to bring about the needed culture change, here are some things you can do to start building the necessary relationships to help you and other change agents make that happen:

- *Volunteer in their organization.* For example, if you want to start a preparedness training initiative at your kid's school, get actively involved at the school. Volunteering your time at PTA/PTO events (or becoming a leader in the organization), helping with fundraising events, tutoring children, and generally helping out around the school are all great ways to show your interest in the organization. It will also help you build relationships with key decision-makers within the organization. For elected officials, this could mean helping out with their campaigns, hosting neighborhood events at your home for your friends and neighbors to come and meet their elected official, and helping them with their various projects.

- *Encourage and thank the key people in the organization regularly.* Without a doubt, some people will see this as simply kissing up to the decision-makers. I'm not talking about showering them with unearned flattery; such superficial efforts are usually seen for what they are. Take a moment to reach out to your City Councilman or school board member and simply say "I just wanted to let you know I really appreciate your service to the community. I know it can be a thankless job at times, but please know that in our home, your efforts are greatly appreciated." Don't ask for anything; don't suggest they take this action or that action. Just thank them for their service. There are human, too, just like us. Most of them receive far more complaints and criticism than they do appreciation. Your kindness will be remembered.

- *Take an interest in their kids.* And again, I'm not talking about a superficial "how are your kids?" inquiry that we are all accustomed to making as a matter of social grace. If you are truly a champion of change and an advocate for preparing citizens to protect them from harm, you are concerned about their kids, and everyone else's for that matter. It's been my experience that people appreciate your interest in them, but they will always remember the support and interest you show in their children. I do this as often as I can, and as a result, I have met some wonderful young people whom I consider friends.

CREATING YOUR OWN PREPAREDNESS SERVICE PROJECT

Changing the culture to incorporate preparedness into our daily lives requires taking action. Think back to those examples discussed earlier. Movements for civil rights, the environment, teen pregnancy reduction, smoking cessation, and AIDS awareness began when motivated people started doing something about it. If you are interested in seeing preparedness culture take hold in America, you will need to take action in your community to help make that happen. We can do that by creating and carrying out our own preparedness service projects.

Much like a civic club service project or a religious mission project, a preparedness service project involves going out into the community or to local institutions and providing training or supplies to improve community preparedness. Remember what Professor Matt Davis said was the most effective way to do that?

What I have found is that taking disaster prep courses increases people's sense of self-efficacy... they begin to feel that there is something they can do or that they have the skills to start taking action. If you can increase self-efficacy, and salience of the problem, you can increase preparedness.

With more community-based programs, we seem to increase people's sense of community, which is another variable that is positively associated with preparedness. People who feel more of a bond to their community are more likely to get involved and to take precautionary actions. If you don't know or like your neighbors or don't trust community officials, it's unlikely you'll participate in strategies they recommend.

As members of the preparedness movement, we need others to join our efforts. We should not just be disciples of the preparedness movement; we need to be its apostles as well.

Are you ready to get started on your preparedness project? Here are some suggestions on how you might proceed.

1. *Find like-minded people who share your passion.* Sometimes you will have to go it alone, at least initially. But if you have a number of friends or acquaintances who can help you shoulder the load in creating your preparedness project, it will certainly make things easier for you.

2. *Decide what preparedness project you want to pursue.* Is this a project at church? School? Community or neighborhood? Defining the project or initiative early on, while building in some flexibility as it morphs and grows, will help you sell your idea to the decision makers.

3. *Calculate costs and resource needs.* So often in these situations, people who are into preparedness...wait for it...fail to prepare a budget! If you are selling your idea to even a receptive audience, they will want to know the costs, both start up and long term. Have estimates, with supporting documentation, to back up your calculations. When you can show how you arrived at your math, you're more likely to convince a skeptical audience.

4. *How will you pay for it?* This is another key question the decision makers will want you to answer. If you can pull money together yourself, this will go much more smoothly. It's hard to say no to the individual or group who says "I'm/we're ready to drop money and time on this project to make it happen." If you aren't in a position to finance the project yourself, I would suggest finding additional donors (like other Champions of Change who are interested in creating a culture of preparedness) or community/civic organizations whose mission is congruent with what you're trying to do. Alternatively, you may want to scale back the project initially so that it's easier to finance it yourself or with a few others.

A side note on this — a number of organizations provide free training along these lines. Fire departments and your community's emergency management agency will have a wealth of resources you may be able to utilize. Do your homework in this regard. Sometimes it's nice to be able to tell the decision makers "We'd like to do a CPR class for students at the school, and local civic organizations have agreed to partner to make the training available for free." Decision makers — especially those of the elected variety — are hesitant to say no to free training made available by civic-minded organizations.

5. *Create your sales pitch and present it to the decision makers.* Be ready to tell them in 30 seconds or less why this is a good idea. Remember my discussion in an earlier chapter of how realtors and other salespeople will use their sales pitch to eliminate as many objections as they can? You need to do the same thing in the pitch. Anticipate what those objections will be and have an answer for them. It may be that you expect them to say it costs too much/takes too much time/they don't have the resources/there's a lot of red tape to go through. Figure out how to address those things, preferably with data and examples showing why those objections are not well founded.

6. *Be tenacious, yet polite.* Stay on them. You may not succeed in selling your idea the first time and to the first person you give your pitch. Trust me on this — I have countless examples of where I've recommended changes to preparedness efforts or other initiatives where my idea initially went nowhere. Only after diplomatically and repeatedly selling the idea to anyone who would listen did the effort get off the ground. If they continue to blow you off, don't be afraid to go pitch the idea to someone else.

Your efforts will go much more smoothly if you can find others within the organization you're lobbying to champion the effort for you. Let's call them *tenacity multipliers*. Suppose you're trying to create a workplace safety initiative at your place of employment. If you're able to convince someone in the organization who may not be a decision maker him or herself but who is a Champion of Change in her or his own right, that individual's imprimatur on your initiative will multiply your own tenacity.

The fine art of persuasion within an organization centers on leverage – namely, your ability to find the appropriate leverage point and apply the correct amount of force to it. I'm not talking about being manipulative. I'm suggesting you find a way to make it more difficult for decision makers to say no to your idea. For example, is there a major donor to an organization that might see things your way and would be willing to suggest to the organization that they consider taking up your initiative? Is there a well-connected community leader who likes the idea of kids at the local school learning how to make their own bug out bags? Is there a church elder who thinks the church should be doing more to help its members prepare for disasters? Getting some of these people on board and having *them* help you sell your idea to the decision makers will greatly multiply your tenacity.

7. *Think long term.* How will this become a sustained effort at the school/ group/church? It is very important that the organization task someone who will carry out the project because they believe in it, rather than because it was simply assigned to them to do. Generating a broader interest over time will make your efforts more sustainable long term. Find folks within the organization who believe in this as strongly as you do to take ownership of it on a day to day basis. Ideally, this project becomes their pet project.

8. *Set up a meeting with all of the key players.* Have an agenda for the meeting. It's critical that you set the tone in the meeting early on – "this can happen efficiently, effectively, and yield great benefits to the participants and the community."

9. *Find your Aaron.* Those who have read the book of Exodus will remember the exchange Moses had with the Lord at the burning bush. The Lord wanted Moses to lead the Israelites from Egypt, but Moses kept coming up with excuses as to why he ought not be tasked with the job. One of his objections was that he wasn't a good public speaker. And so

the Lord told him he would send Aaron with him to speak on his behalf. [146] If you are like Moses and aren't keen on speaking to groups or even individuals in a persuasive manner, find your Aaron to help you with that.

10. *Apply more tenacity if you aren't making headway.* It may take more than one effort to launch this within an organization. At some point, you may decide to move on from that organization and offer to help another organization get your initiative off the ground. Just because a local civic organization doesn't want to undertake your initiative doesn't mean another one across town wouldn't.

11. *Attend and participate in the project.* It's not enough to be the "money person" or the "idea person" initiating the effort. You need to be actively involved seeing it through. Your engagement creates accountability for those implementing it. It also gives you some insight as to what portions of your initiative work well and which ones need further refinement.

12. *Follow up regularly.* What's the next thing you need to keep momentum moving forward? If you're investing time and money into a project to help others, it's reasonable for you to ask questions to see that things are getting done. Well-meaning people get busy, and sometimes things fall through the cracks. Following up with those tasked to implement the program will help hold them accountable and keep them on track.

13. *Get past participants to be your acolytes.* For example, think about the kids who came through that program you created at their school to teach them basic first aid and preparedness. Did any of those kids ever have to use their training to help someone? Find that kid and make them your poster child for future efforts. It's one thing for us to say "this training initiative is great and it's free," but it's another to have that past participant say "I took the training and helped save lives using what I learned in the course." The latter testimony is worth far more than any sales pitch you can make.

14. *Repeat your efforts.* So you convinced your local civic organization to help prepare low income individuals for possible disasters. Great! Take that effort to another organization or to another part of town. Using the

lessons you've learned, replicate your efforts in other initiatives. (By now, hopefully, you have been able to get a number of people on board with your efforts, so they can be a big help in doing this.)

Let me share with you some examples of efforts you might undertake, along with a game plan on how to go about it. These are just templates; you should feel free to modify your approach as you see fit.

EMERGENCY RESPONSE TRAINING FOR STUDENTS AT A LOCAL HIGH SCHOOL.

This project was one my larger efforts at creating a culture of preparedness. I shared my story with you earlier in the chapter. I'm going to provide you with a more generic template to give you some ideas on how you might do something similar in your neighborhood's schools.

Once you figure out the specifics of the project – a program to provide high school students taking a health class to receive CPR and first aid training, perhaps – you will need to work through the steps I previously shared with you. In this situation, I would prefer to make the pitch with the provider of the training – the local emergency medical service (EMS) department, for example. Once you've figured out the costs and how it's going to be financed, you will need to determine the best way to get the local high school on board with your effort.

For a public high school, I would contact the school principal or the health teacher about the idea and set up a meeting to discuss it further. Before that meeting, I would want to sit down with the EMS representative who will attend the meeting with me to go over our sales pitch, identify objections, and come up with ways to eliminate them.

During the meeting with the school leaders, I'd give my entire pitch – limiting it to two minutes – and then let the EMS person add additional details to the discussion. I'd then conclude by "asking for the business" as salespeople do and say "We'd like to see your school – the only school in the city, as best we can tell – receive this free opportunity to teach life-saving skills. Is this

something we could start next semester?" At that point, the decision maker –
most likely the principal – might tell you it's a great idea, but that: a) the class
curriculum is extensive and thus doesn't leave time for such training and/or
b) they would have to get approval from the local school superintendent to do
something like this.

Your job at that point is to smile thoughtfully and have a response ready to
go. My response to that (since I would have already done my homework) would
be something like this:

*I certainly appreciate the need to meet curriculum demands and to get the ap-
provals from school district administrators. I would add to those concerns you've
mentioned a couple of others. First, God forbid there's a school shooting here.
Part of this training would be to help kids help each other in the event the unthinkable happens. Or maybe it's a bus crash on the way to a school event. Or a
tornado hits the school and first responders are so overwhelmed with the disaster
that it takes an hour to reach us. Or maybe it's an emergency away from school
where your students can save someone's life. Your kids can be trained to deal with
that.*

*Second, I get the sense from talking to Sally Smith and Joe Jones – two
of the school board members of this school district – that this is <u>precisely</u>
the sort of thing we should be teaching our kids. They were really excited to
hear that the EMS and a local civic group are willing to work with this particular school and provide this training to our kids at no cost to taxpayers. I
don't think you'll have much trouble getting the requisite approval from the
superintendent.*

*The school is always asking parents and citizens to get involved with the
school. Well, here we are. How can we help the school and its students get better
prepared for emergencies?*

Did I name drop there? Absolutely. And how did I know Sally Smith and Joe
Jones were on board with this? Because a couple of weeks before this meeting,
the EMS employee and I took them to lunch to discuss it with them. We already

had the tenacity multipliers on board with us before we pitched the idea to the initial decision maker.

I might mention that conversation with Sally and Joe in my sales pitch rather than holding in reserve to address objections. I may even mention the whole "get your kids prepared for a bus crash or school shooter" angle in my sales pitch. It really depends on the situation and how responsive the school principal is to the initial pitch. That's a judgment call.

The decision maker may have an even better idea — partnering with an existing program to expand it or to help make it more available to more students. Should they offer that option, it's a good sign. Integrating training into an existing program is often easier than creating the program from scratch. If I'm able to get the school to buy into this, I want to keep the momentum and schedule regular follow up meetings or conference calls. These are busy people. If they know you are remaining engaged, they will do the same.

Many people are keen on good ideas, but often they fail for lack of execution. To avoid that, suggest to the key players that everyone agree on certain deadlines to get things done. In this case, you might ask the school principal how long they think it will take for the school superintendent to sign off on the project. Note that on your calendar to follow-up with the principal. (You'll also want to circle back with people like Sally and Joe to let them know how the meeting went and to see if they can do anything to expedite the process.)

Once the project begins and the training is being provided, arrange to attend one of the training sessions. School officials need to see community activists and parents involved on campus. They need our support, and one way we can provide that is to get involved on campus and then let school board and other school district leadership know what a great job the teachers and administrators of the school are doing. You being there and taking ownership of the project, building relationships with key school personnel and leadership, and setting an example for others in the community to follow will greatly enhance the culture of preparedness in that school.

CREATING A PREPAREDNESS PROGRAM WITHIN A CHURCH OR OTHER PLACE OF WORSHIP

Houses of worship may seem like odd places to start developing a culture of preparedness. Yet for many reasons they are ideal venues for this initiative.

There are roughly 350,000 religious congregations in the United States."[147] When you think about the roles that religious institutions and local congregations play in disaster recovery, it's easy to see why these institutions have a vested interest in seeing that people in their congregations and communities are prepared for a wide spectrum of perils. Houses of worship are not immune from evil; my wife attended her concealed handgun license class with a pastor who was taking the class due to an increase in church robberies during services.

As discussed earlier, many people of faith believe that there is a strong biblical commandment to be prepared. Such an ethos can help launch this initiative in those churches which adhere to that. Regardless of what religious text a house of worship uses or how they interpret it, religious institutions in the United States have traditionally been on the front line after a disaster.[148] This is simply a logical extension of that effort.

How might we utilize our houses of worship as cultural change platforms?

Ask yourself if you are a member of a house of worship where such an initiative would be well received. Most modern day Christian churches have a wide range of cultures and interests within their own congregations. In some churches, creating a culture of preparedness would not be a high priority. That's not to say you cannot create one within your own house of worship; the effort will be easier in some houses than others.

If you are attending a house of worship where you believe such an effort would be well received by at least some of the members, you are off to a good start. Perhaps your next step is to go about identifying people who will help you champion the effort. You can post notices in the weekly bulletin about an upcoming informational meeting to discuss the church's readiness for various disasters. Those who attend that meeting are likely your champions of change. As we discussed earlier, those who show up to do the work generally get the result they want.

When we talk about creating preparedness initiatives within a house of worship, there are a number of different directions the conversation can go. We could be talking about an initiative to preserve the continuity of religious services after a disaster – protecting the physical structure of the church, synagogue, mosque or temple – and its ability to continue to meet the needs of its members. We might be talking about efforts to help the members affected by a disaster or emergency. Additionally, we could be talking about helping members of the organization get better prepared so that they are less likely to need the temporal resources of the organization. One of your early chores will be to determine which of these directions you wish to take. You may choose to do more than one.

Ask yourself and your team:

- What exactly do we want to do? Are we going to create an awareness campaign in our church to get people prepared? Are we going to host seminars on how to go about it? Can we have the worship leader stress the need for preparedness in their coming messages to the congregation? Are we going to focus on our organization's ability to better respond to the needs of the community after disaster? Spend adequate time sorting out these details and refining your goals.
- What resources will you need? Who will pay for them? These are critical questions that deserve a fair amount of your time.
- Who will make your pitch to the organization's leadership? As we discussed in the school scenario earlier, if you can get someone in the organization's leadership on board with your efforts before you make the pitch, it can dramatically cut down on resistance you may face.
- Once we get the requisite approvals, how can we keep up the momentum and execution of the plan? This is where your calendar, regular meetings, and follow up emails and phone calls come in. It bears repeating again: many good ideas die for lack of execution. If your team is convinced that the proposed preparedness project is a good fit for your house of worship, don't let the effort languish.

I highly encourage you to do some online research into the efforts of other houses of worship to create a culture of preparedness. In my community, churches often work together through the Austin Disaster Relief Network to provide preparedness training and disaster relief to local residents.

Another way to foster a preparedness culture is to utilize a religious organization's mission efforts to improve the readiness of those they serve. For example, my church regularly sends its high school-aged members on mission trips to help low-income individuals make necessary repairs to their homes. I thought this would be a great opportunity to provide some much-needed preparedness supplies to those who are in need.

The first thing I did was to make a donation to the mission trip fund to help finance the overall effort. I did not place any restrictions on the donation; mission leaders could use the money however they saw fit. I simply wanted to demonstrate my thanks and support for the efforts of those going on the mission trip. Contributions have an additional effect: they help build relationships with those who are taking time out of their lives to put the effort together. When they see that you are supportive of their overall effort, they're more likely to engage with you in a discussion about preparedness.

I then reached out to one of the leaders of the mission trip, a good friend of mine who is in my Sunday school class. I asked whether I could donate smoke detectors to be installed by his team in the homes they were helping to repair. He graciously agreed.

You can imagine the size of the box that showed up on our front doorstep with 50 smoke detectors! Because this initiative stemmed from our faith, my stepdaughter and I carefully removed each detector from the box and wrote "Psalms 121:7" on the back of each one. That verse reads, "The Lord keeps you from all harm and watches over your life."

Mission trips are highly effective platforms for creating a culture of preparedness. In the one I just described, not only do the recipients see these churchgoing young people installing life safety devices in their homes (thus reinforcing the message with the recipients that the Lord cares for them and wants them to be prepared), the young people themselves see preparedness being made a priority by their own church. It's an opportunity to educate two completely separate demographics simultaneously. If handing out smoke detectors with Bible verses written on the backs of them is what it takes to help create a culture of preparedness here in Texas, I will gladly buy more smoke detectors for our church youth group to install.

These are just a few examples of how institutions of faith can help move the needle and create a more prepared America. I suspect you and your fellow believers can come together, prayerfully, and discern many other effective ways to do so.

GETTING YOUR HOA, COMMUNITY GROUP OR WORKPLACE TO BE BETTER PREPARED

We've just discussed two examples of how you might go about starting a preparedness initiative in your neighborhood schools or houses of worship. Those same steps you use in those venues can be used in other venues, including your neighborhood associations or community groups.

You might consider some of these examples of ways to help get these groups prepared:

- *Neighborhood fire drill contest.* Who can get their families out quickest? Who has a predetermined spot for their family to meet? Which family has the most working smoke detectors in their home? Who has a fire extinguisher in their home? In their vehicle? Your neighborhood association can set up some basic rules for the contest and come up with prizes for the winners. Some friendly neighbor versus neighbor competition is a healthy way to motivate people to get prepared.

- *Local fire department-sponsored fire extinguisher training for your group.* Here's a secret to getting fire fighters to really, really like you: ice cream. When I was a volunteer fire fighter years ago, and a citizen came by to drop off a gallon of ice cream to those on duty that day, you can rest assured we remembered not only the name of the person who brought it, but also their address. Those residents who made a local habit of it quickly became fire fighter favorites. And when the alarm sounded for an address that even sounded closely similar to the one of the Ice Cream Fairy, there was an added level of urgency to get on scene.

Build a relationship with your local fire department. Take them some ice cream and invite them to attend your neighborhood or community event to provide fire extinguisher training for the adults and fire safety training for the kids. Many of the larger fire departments have access to a tremendous amount of educational resources for the community. They have goals to meet, too, which often involve doing events like those.

- *First aid training day*. A number of organizations, from local scouting groups to the Red Cross, can provide your neighborhood or community with basic first aid training. The odds that you will need to know how to treat a serious cut or other injury are far greater than the odds that you will need to use a weapon to defend your life. Preparedness is about executing the basics well, and first aid training is clearly one of the basic skills.

- *Pet preparedness day.* Pet preparedness is a fast growing body of literature within the preparedness community. Knowing how to do basic first aid for Fluffy or Fido can help your pet tremendously. Further, making basic preparations, including having medical records, an emergency food supply, and other pet needs ready to go can greatly reduce the stress on both you and your furry family member. A number of veterinarian clinics and veterinary schools do presentations on the subject on a regular basis.

- *Safety fair at your workplace*. My former employer's workplace safety committee – yes, that existed even before I joined the company – sponsored a safety fair for employees every year. Vendors came in to sell life safety equipment such as fire extinguishers and smoke detectors, as well as to talk about various training opportunities and to share safety and preparedness advice with employees. It was one of the best attended employee events of the year.

- *Preparedness seminars at work.* Will your business or employer be up and running immediately after an emergency? Some industries have an obligation to be back online and running after a catastrophe. One company I know of encourages its employees to have several months of food, water and other necessities stored up for the entire family. This business keeps additional food stores, generators and fuel on hand to keep the office running. Employees are told that they will have 72 hours after an emergency to deal with the situation and then get back to work if they can reasonably do so, as the company expects to deal with a large increase of business obligations after a crisis. Has your company determined how it will maintain a competitive advantage after a crisis? Has it determined how it will serve existing customers? These are conversations that you can have with your company's leadership that could put you on a trajectory to be a magnificent Champion of Change in your workplace.

- *Using MeetUp and other social media platforms to create groups for sharing skills and ideas.* It's never been easier to connect with people of similar interests than it is in today's virtually connected society. Forming your own group to help others learn (and to learn some new skills yourself!) is a great way to create a new culture of readiness. I've created my own informal group of preppers who meet four or five times a year to discuss preparedness tips, gear and issues. It's a great way to get new ideas and socialize with like-minded folks.

As you can see, there are endless possibilities when it comes to creating events to help others prepare. You can easily combine a number of these into a single event, or you could offer some of these opportunities at a local county fair, farmer's market, street festival, or any other event where there are a number of people.

This may seem like a daunting task. Some may be hesitant to try some of the things I've outlined, fearing failure, poor attendance, inefficient use of resources, or uncertainty on how to get started or who to call. Here's the good news: it's really, really hard to screw this up. That's the truth. When you do make mistakes, they will be learning experiences, helping you plan the next event much more effectively. I've helped put on a number of events and initiatives over the years, some of which were wildly successful and others which were a complete bust.

The worst thing that can happen is that you take no action whatsoever. So what if only a handful of people show up? Did you learn a new skill at the event? Did you build new relationships with experts? Did you meet some new friends who share your interest in the subjects? *Let that be your measure of success.* While it would be great to teach CPR to every high school student in your community, have every adult trained on how to use a fire extinguisher, and for every pet owner to have a bug out bag for their critters, it is going to take a long time to change the culture sufficiently to get to that point. Just do what you can, learn the lessons of your efforts, and become one of the Champions of Change desperately needed within our movement.

FINAL THOUGHTS ABOUT THE CHAMPIONS OF CHANGE

This brings us to a question that many of you are probably asking yourselves right about now: how do I deal with the risk of being viewed as a nut job by encouraging people to get better prepared? (If you were not thinking of that question, by all means do not let me put that idea into your head... just skip ahead to the next paragraph.) I can assure you that you are going to have critics. I've had a number of them over the years, telling me and others that I was paranoid, a fear monger, and perhaps even mentally unstable. I learned long ago I cannot win over the hearts and minds of every single person. No one can. However, if more and more of us take an interest in promoting this, we will begin to make it culturally acceptable to have these conversations and to get our country more self-reliant and less reliant on aid from others during a crisis.

My dad tells a story of being in an Army ROTC class in college. At that time, he had no plans to join the military, although a few years later he served as an Army dental officer, concluding with a tour in Vietnam. He once told me that even if he had not gone into the Army right after dental school, the skills he learned in his ROTC class were phenomenal — crisis leadership, basic survival skills, learning how to use a map and compass, first aid, and several others. Who among us would be harmed by learning skills like this? Would we be a weaker country if more citizens had these skills? Or would we all be better off if we had a modicum of training, skills and knowledge on how to manage short-term and long-term crises in our lives?

About 12 years ago, I made the decision to "out" myself as a prepper. Despite a fair amount of criticism from other well-meaning preppers, I did so in large part because I felt like there needed to be a voice – a transparent voice – getting the message out. While I'm not critical of those leaders in the cause who use *nom de plumes* or speak vaguely about where they live or work, I do think there is a place for some of us within the movement to use our real name, identify the city where we live, and make ourselves available to talk face-to-face with those who want to learn more about what we are doing. If we are going to create a culture of preparedness in America, people need to see others setting an example of it. Right or wrong, it is the decision that I have made, because I believe it is the best one for me.

You might say that you don't have time, money or other resources to lead your own effort. Do you think our Founding Fathers had unlimited finances and resources to donate to our nation? Did those model citizens who manned the nation's Civil Defense efforts have a limitless bank account and ample free time? Do those brave people who staff our nation's network of volunteer fire departments and medical first responder teams have other demands on their time and assets? They were limited in resources, just like us. Yet these individuals did not let their personal situation keep them from their mission to make America better and more resilient. If you believe as I do that we should build a culture of preparedness in America, we need to be willing to devote some of our resources to make the change we seek.

While we can only hope that the day will come where celebrities and national thought leaders will take up their own initiatives to create a preparedness culture, for now we have to be realistic. The cultural movements I discussed in the very beginning of this chapter often had very humble roots, and yet they become mainstays in our nation's culture today. I am confident that if ordinary folks like you and me create a culture where preparedness is a result of good citizenship, others will follow.

Become a Champion of Change and help us create a preparedness culture in our country. Figure out how you can best do that, find your mission, and move forward. And part of being that facilitator of change to create that culture is getting prepared yourself. What's the best way to do that?

PIVOT POINTS:

- Champions of Change are the people who make things happen. Any of us willing to roll up our sleeves and engage on a preparedness project can be a Champion of Change.
- Being an effective culture changer doesn't require us to reinvent the wheel. There are plenty of opportunities all around us where we can start building the readiness culture and get others to join our efforts. Some of the best ideas are created by simply sitting down with a notepad and just writing down ideas as they come to mind. Pick the best two or three on the list.
- The formula for success as a Champion of Change:
  - Formulate a plan
  - Anticipate objections
  - Take action
  - Follow up
  - Repeat

PREPARE NOW

O n a flight home after a particularly long business trip one evening, I sketched an outline of what would be covered in this book. This chapter was not in it.

I mentioned in an earlier chapter than we do not need more books on how to become better prepared. And I stand by that assertion. Which means it's a bit inconsistent for me to create a "how to" chapter for this book.

I have read a fair number of books on preparedness, and in reading on line reviews of these books, I've noticed a trend. People who buy books on this subject expect the author to provide them with preparedness guidance, even if the author clearly states the book isn't a how-to book.

That used to strike me as odd. But as I got to know people who are just beginning their preparedness efforts, it became very apparent that people are overwhelmed at the process. Many simply don't know where to start. Handing them a to-do list and a to-purchase list often increases their angst. Most of us cannot quit our job and enroll in a full time preparedness program for several months. Nor can we spend thousands of dollars on supplies to get us better prepared.

Shopping lists and to dos will only get us so far. We need a routine or schedule to help us prioritize and set a sustainable pace by which we acquire the assets and skills we need.

In Austin, we have a large number of people who are always training for some sort of athletic event: marathons, triathlons, long distance bike rides, and amateur mixed martial arts contests. I quickly learned how many of these athletes train for their upcoming events. They follow a training schedule.

Training schedules are a dime a dozen. You can do an internet search and come up with countless training routines and schedules to get you read for the big day. Provided you're able to stick to the schedule, you can in fact get conditioned to finish a marathon with only a few months of training. It's pretty remarkable when you think about it.

By creating and sticking to a readiness schedule, you can manage your "to do" and "to buy" lists on an orderly, sustainable pace. Absent an imminent threat, we are not required to obtain everything we need for a long term crisis in just three days. If we pace ourselves over a year's time, the burden and resulting stress level will be much lower.

Before we get into the readiness schedule, we need to review a few important items that will make your efforts much easier. Those training for a marathon take care of some preliminary items before they begin their training runs. Nutrition, hydration, stretching, a physician's approval – all of those things need to be resolved before the actual training begins. So we're going to get a few things squared away before we start our schedule as well.

The information I am going to share with you took me over a decade to acquire. I've made many mistakes in my preparedness efforts over the years, and the guidance in the coming pages are in part the result of my failures. It's my hope you can learn from these and not make the mistakes I made.

HOW TO PAY FOR IT

Even when we prepare on the cheap, it still costs money. Unless you have substantial resources, you should determine how you will go about paying for your purchases and training.

Set your preparedness budget before you set your readiness schedule. How much can you afford to spend per month on your efforts? And where in your overall budget can you shift money around to pay for it?

I've heard unfortunate stories of people financing their acquisitions. Going into debt to pay for your efforts is rarely a good idea. Credit card interest rates can easily eat away at your income, making an otherwise stable financial situation a precarious one. Don't plan on financing your preparedness efforts. Pay cash for everything. And if you're in debt with high interest credit cards, I would strongly suggest you make eliminating it your top preparedness priority. Some of the ideas in the following paragraphs may help with that.

How can you find money to help defray the costs? I have a few strategies in mind, all of which I have personally used. By far the best way to pay for your efforts is to become your own financial plumber. No, you won't need to actually become a real plumber (although based on what I've had to pay my plumber from time to time, it's clear to me that plumbing is a great occupation for financial and career independence.)

Pull out the last three months of bank statements and credit card statements and identify the "cash leaks" – those recurring or frequent charges you have in your budget that yield little to no benefit to you. Do you have a membership to some club you never use? Are you subscribed to an internet site that gives you access through a paywall for content that you never access? Are you spending too much at the local convenience store on diet sodas? (The guy staring back at me in the mirror is really bad about that.) Once you've identified them, be your own financial plumber and fix the leaks. Get those automatically recurring charges shut off. Write down how much per month those were costing you. That money just became a part of your preparedness budget.

What about other things you use or do but don't really need? Do you really need hundreds of cable channels with premium upgrades? Do you really need to eat out that often? Figure out where you can cut back. Add the money you are spending on those monthly expenses to your preparedness budget.

Next, clean out your closets, garage and storage units. (If you can empty your storage unit, take the money you were paying for rental and add that to your preparedness budget.) We all have stuff in these places we never use. Much of it may be worth something to someone else. List it for sale on eBay, Craig's List, and other media. This strategy has two benefits – you're coming up with cash for your preparedness efforts, and at the same time you're making room for things like long term food storage you will acquire over the next year.

Here's a way to get Uncle Sam to help you pay for your preparations, provided your CPA agrees with you. When you begin to make your purchases for those long term storable foods that can be used regularly in non-emergency situations – things like instant soups, peanut butter, macaroni and cheese, pastas, and other foods useful to food banks – make sure you keep the receipts. Track on the expiration dates of your stored foods, and before these reach their "best by" dates, take them to your local house of worship or food pantry and donate them. Make sure the charity gives you a receipt for tax purposes. Attach your purchase receipt to your donation receipt (and maybe a picture of your donation.) Assuming you are in a taxable income position to take a charitable deduction, your tax deduction just subsidized your next purchase of fresh disaster foods, and it enabled you to be a blessing to a needy family!

PRIORITIZATION

Many people get into preparedness primarily to rationalize their purchases of various pieces of gear. Purchases of guns, ammo, generators, and other gadgets can easily be justified by claiming they are part of your efforts to become self-reliant. If that's all you buy, and if you don't train with your gear, you aren't really prepping. You are simply rationalizing purchases you wanted to make anyway.

We need certain things to survive. Air, food, water and shelter are at the top of the list. You can't eat ammo, and electrical generators don't purify water. In the pages that follow, I have created the order of acquisition based on priorities, rather than what's cool to have.

Take it from me, a once novice prepper who bought stuff because it looked cool rather than it being a priority. Prioritization is key if you want to prepare in a cost effective manner.

TWO THINGS YOU MUST DO BEFORE YOU SPEND MONEY ON PREPAREDNESS ITEMS

This won't be fun, but it is necessary. First, make sure you have a will and other estate planning documents completed in full. I realize that's not as exciting as buying a really nice survival gadget, but in the bigger scheme of things, you likely won't need to report your GPS coordinates with a satellite phone to search and rescue technicians. Everyone, however, assumes room temperature at some point. Where will your assets go when that happens? If you have minor children from a previous relationship, who will manage those assets — like your life insurance and retirement funds -for them until they are adults? (If you don't decide, the court will likely allow the kids' other parent to do that. Are you okay with that?) Who will make the decision to end life support for you? How much life support do you want, anyway? A lawyer who regularly drafts standard wills and trusts can help you with this for a few hundred dollars.

Second, you need to sit down with your insurance agent and thoroughly review all of your coverages to ensure that you have the right policies in place. I understand that's not very exciting and can be rather costly when it comes to adding additional premiums. As a lawyer who has counseled numerous people after the death of a loved one or after a catastrophic disaster, I can tell you first hand you do not want to find out that you lack adequate insurance when you need it most. Do you or your spouse need life insurance in case one of you dies unexpectedly? Do you have adequate health insurance? If your house were to burn down tonight, what would be covered? How much would your deductible be? If your car is struck by an uninsured motorist on the way home from work, how much coverage would you have for medical bills, lost wages, and pain and suffering? What about insurance for long term care (for extended nursing home expenses) and disability insurance (to replace the income you lose due to an extended illness)?

And if you are a business owner, please make sure that your business insurance policy includes something called *business interruption coverage*. This critical coverage provides you with money to replace your lost revenue as a result of a disaster. Adding this coverage to your business policy often adds very little additional premium. It's a very critical coverage that will make your recovery much easier if you have it.

AVOID THE URGE TO SKIP AHEAD IN THE READINESS SCHEDULE

"Oh look! Paul says I need to buy some guns. I'll get those now rather than waiting."

Don't do that.

It may be tempting —and it may even give you some peace of mind — to skip ahead and learn a new skill or buy a new tool before you have secured more basic items. As the marathon participant doesn't skip ahead in the training schedule, nor should we. Our efforts need to be sustainable, and when we skip ahead, we reduce the sustainability of our efforts.

If you do come to a part of the readiness schedule where you can honestly say, "I have all of these things already," then by all means move on to the next month ahead of schedule.

GIVE THE GIFT OF PREPAREDNESS

This may not go over well with everyone in your family, but my family knows it goes over well with me. I regularly manage to get preparedness toys and gift cards to my favorite preparedness suppliers during the holidays. I've received grain mills, solar ovens, solar cookers, shortwave radios, backpacks, and other supplies over the years. For those in your household who don't mind getting prepper gear or gift certificates to training courses, using the gift giving season as a way to help you meet your preparedness goals can be quite effective. Just make sure the recipient of your preparedness gift really wants that grain mill or new ham radio.

THE TYPES OF SUPPLIES YOU NEED

One of the big challenges you will have is determining what types of items to purchase. For example, if I were to recommend you set aside a week's worth of food, what would you buy to do that? Freeze dried meals? More of the same items you normally consume? Buckets of grains, beans, and powdered milk? If I suggest you acquire a reliable rifle, what brand and model would you get?

I'll provide some guidance along the way, but I encourage you to do your own research into your purchases. Above all else, make sure you:

- Buy quality. Cheap isn't necessarily better, especially if you want your gear to work reliably when things are bad.
- Buy things that are easily repaired with readily available parts. You might not choose to buy some exotic firearm for home defense when an AR-15 or Remington 870 shotgun – very common guns with readily available parts – would do just as well.
- Buy value. When it comes to foods, make sure you are getting the most bang for your buck. That means you're buying nutrient dense foods. On the food tracking spreadsheet I created for my own use, I calculated the ratio of dollars to protein for each item, as protein is by far the most expensive nutrient you will need to acquire. Pay extra attention to the details when buying your food. I once ordered a "30 day supply of food" for one person, and when I did the math based on a 2,000 calorie/50 grams of protein per day diet, I found the 30 day supply would only feed me about 14 days.

A NOTE ABOUT STORABLE FOODS

Few topics in preparedness raise as many questions as how best to create a food storage program. This is another area in which you will want to spend some time researching to make sure you make the right decision for your family. To help you get started in your research, I'll offer a few pointers:

- Understand the difference between freeze dried and dehydrated foods. Freeze dried is generally more expensive and has better nutritional retention. Dehydrated foods are generally cheaper…and are more familiar to us. Pasta, rice, and dried beans are just some examples of dehydrated foods we eat on a regular basis.
- Note that the popular MRE meals are loaded in sodium and have a limited shelf life. These meals are great for bugging out, but they can leave something to be desired long term. Due to their sodium content, you need adequate hydration when eating them. They tend to be rather expensive compared to freeze dried or dehydrated foods.

- When buying storable foods from a vendor, buy a small amount and taste test it before making a major purchase from that vendor. You don't want to spend thousands of dollars on a storable food system only to find out you hate the taste of a certain vendor's food or certain items in their inventory. A minimal purchase will tell you much about the product you're considering.

Taking advantage of sales and coupons

I'm going to deviate from the conventional wisdom. But you need to hear it nonetheless: *just because something is on sale or is a good deal doesn't mean you should buy it at that particular moment.* My local big box outdoor retailer regularly sends me coupons and flyers in the mail – "Save $100 on a $500 purchase" – which is a great way to stock up on things I might want. But do I really need those items at the moment? More often than not, I don't. Again, stick to the readiness schedule. Spending $800 dollars on an alternative energy system that is on sale when you only have two weeks of food set aside isn't the best use of resources.

Determining where to put all of this stuff

One of our biggest challenges is figuring out where we're going to keep our food storage and other supplies. Earlier I mentioned the need to clean out your closets and storage units. This will certainly free up some space. Look underneath your beds as well. Is there any wasted shelf space in your kitchen?

Some people have become quite creative in making storage space for their supplies. I recommend you do some Internet research to come up with cost effective ways to do so.

A few thoughts about using rented storage units as a place to park your supplies are in order. I have experimented with this off and on, and I've come to the realization that using a storage unit may be necessary for some families. Ideally, when looking for a storage unit, choose one that is:

- climate controlled
- preferably on the first floor (so that you don't need an elevator to get your supplies out when things get bad)
- managed by a company which aggressively treats for bugs and vermin
- in a building with lots of concrete walls for protection from the elements and electromagnetic pulse (EMP) exposure if you're storing electronics in there.

Note that many storage unit companies prohibit the storage of food. If you're planning to do so anyway, I would recommend using food grade plastic buckets with high quality lids. This will discourage most if not all critters. I also aggressively use my own bug spray and glue traps in storage units, in addition to what the storage company uses.

One other option which may be available to you, that while a bit pricey may save you money long term, is a small storage shed in the backyard. It can be a game changer when it comes to creating storage space. When we had ours built, we specified a place in the wall where we could install a small air conditioner. While we don't store food in our shed, we could if we needed to, especially if we ran the AC during the warm months. Do the math – a shed investment may be a better deal long term than renting space from a storage company.

RESEARCHING THINGS ALONG THE WAY

I am devoting a single chapter to a subject matter others have written entire books about. I won't be able to cover all of the details; that's not my goal. You'll need to research things along the way, in large part so you will know exactly what you are buying and if it's right for your situation.

If you need suggested readings to jump start your efforts, I highly recommend these three:

- *Crisis Preparedness Handbook: A Comprehensive Guide to Home Storage and Physical Survival,* by Jack Spigarelli
- *Ragnar's Urban Survival,* by Ragnar Benson

- *How to Survive the End of the World as We Know* It, by James Wesley Rawles

These inexpensive books will provide you with a wealth of information about the details of how to prepare. Read and study them. Jack Spigarelli's book may provide better guidance on building a food storage plan than any other book out there. Ragnar Benson has a tremendous amount of real world experience to share with readers. James Wesley Rawles represents the next generation of preparedness writers; he brings a full spectrum approach to the preparedness effort.

THE BOTTOM LINE – WHAT IS ALL OF THIS GOING TO COST ME?

As I said earlier, it's not cheap. But it doesn't have to be expensive. Most of us are already spending money on things we don't really need, like fancy cable television packages, time shares, nicer than necessary vehicles, boats and other toys. Make preparedness a priority in your life, and you will find the money to make it happen. And the good news is this – once you have your preparedness affairs in order, the ongoing expense to maintain them (rotating the food, preventative maintenance on certain items) will be minimal. Once you've achieved that basic level of preparedness, you can get right back to spending eight dollars a day at Starbucks while watching 500 channels on your big screen television, if you so choose.

The costs will vary in large part on how prepared you already are, and how many people you're preparing for. A large family will certainly require more expense than a young couple without children. The food expenses – likely your biggest expense – will vary greatly on whether you choose to buy staples such as whole grains, beans, powdered milk, and rice in bulk, or if you want the convenience (and added expense) of freeze dried meals. Just to give you a ball park, expect to spend between $120 to $300 per person for a month's worth of food. The low end of the range assumes you are buying staples in bulk; the high end assumes you're buying a year's supply of freeze dried meals that only require you to add hot water and stir. The choice is yours; both strategies work well in the end. Companies like Emergency Essentials (beprepared.com) have programs allowing you to set a monthly budget for food purchase. They will then bill you monthly for a set amount and send you items that fit your budget and your nutritional needs.

Some of the months in the readiness schedule will be more expensive than others, especially in the early portion of the schedule. You may decide to take a month or two to build up some cash before you start the schedule; I think this is a great idea. While you're setting aside cash to help you get started, use that time to research products so that when it comes time to acquire them, you will know what you need to purchase and who has the best prices for it.

What if you aren't spending money on niceties and don't have closets filled with stuff you don't need? What if your budget is simply so lean that you cannot realistically acquire preparedness supplies and training?

There are some good internet articles and books on preparing on a tight budget. I would suggest you spend some time researching those options. Could you plan on sheltering with friends or family members who are into prepared-ness and are sympathetic to your situation? Some frugal people plan to ride out a disaster's aftermath with others who are in a position to meet their physi-cal needs in exchange for help around the house before and during the crisis. Pooling resources with others would allow you to join in on bulk purchases to save money. This problem requires some creative thinking on your part, but it is not insurmountable.

THE TRAINING SCHEDULE

In the following pages, I outline a system to go from "I'm not prepared" to "I have a basic level of readiness" in a year's time. You can accelerate the plan if you wish, provided you take things in the order I outline below.

And what's so special about the order I recommend? You will quickly notice I place great emphasis on getting food, water and emergency funds squared away before anything else. The odds you will need to prepare a meal without elec-tricity are greater than the odds you will need to shoot at bandits raiding homes in your neighborhood. Like in sports, we need to execute the basics well. In preparedness, starvation and dehydration are basic problems we want to avoid.

If you cannot meet the goals in the timeframes I suggest, don't worry. Just work towards them as best you can. Once you complete a month's worth of goals, even if it takes three months, then move on to the next month's goals. Don't get discouraged. This is not a race!

MONTH ONE

- Cash to cover one week's worth of basic living expenses. (You will need to keep your cash supply at home, in a safe place. Do not rely on your local ATM to be functioning after an emergency or your local bank to let you access your safe deposit box.)
- Food for one week.
- Toilet paper and paper towels for three months.
- Water (absolute minimum of one gallon per day, per person; two gallons per day is better) for two weeks. This can be in the form of gallon jugs, five gallon camping jugs, a rainwater storage system or swimming pool. Don't forget that you have several gallons of water in your water heater which can be tapped in an emergency. (You'll need to go online and see how best to drain it; it's a very easy process that even a child can do.)
- A basic supply of first aid materials and over-the-counter medications your family frequently uses.
- Exercise: begin walking three miles, three times a week.

MONTH TWO

- Food for an additional week.
- Pet food for six months.
- An alternative energy method to cook (small propane stove or burner with fuel to run it, for example).

- An LED flashlight or headlamp for each member of the family, with spare batteries.
- A NOAA weather radio. Get a programmable one so you can set the alerts just for your county and for the threats you want to know about.
- Exercise: walk five miles, three times a week or other similar exercise along those lines.
- Health: if you need to lose weight, begin dieting. I find the Weight Watchers program to be the easiest, most effective and sustainable one out there. My wife and I have both had excellent results with that program.
- Resources for purifying water. There are a number of options here. We use a Berkey water filtration system at our house. I highly recommend it.
- Water for two weeks.

MONTH THREE

- Food for an additional week.
- Two portable and reliable AM/FM radios with spare batteries.
- Develop a basic rainwater collection system. If you live somewhere that makes that impossible or impractical, determine alternative sources of water and practice gathering it from those locations– nearby streams, lakes, ponds, or community swimming pools - and then taking it home without using a gasoline powered vehicle.
- Exercise: begin some form of resistance training, whether that is using weights at the gym or doing an at-home program.

MONTH FOUR

- Cash for an additional one half week's worth of living expenses.
- Food for an additional month.
- Exercise: continue with cardio and resistance training.

MONTH FIVE

- Food for an additional month
- One month's supply of water.
- Cash for an additional one half week's worth of expenses.
- Exercise: continue with cardio and resistance training.

MONTH SIX

- Food for an additional month.
- Exercise: continue with cardio and resistance training.
- Primary home defense firearm and the means to secure it, such as a lock box or gun safe. This needs to be either a rifle or shotgun, made by a reputable manufacturer, in a popular model and caliber. We want to purchase "popular" models and calibers not so that we fit in with the cool kids, but because the ammunition and spare parts are commonly available. You will need to research the options best for you; many books and articles have been written about this subject. At the end of the day, if you stick to one of the following firearms on this list, you meet all of the criteria above:
    - Mossberg 500, 590 or 930 shotgun, in either 12 gauge or 20 gauge
    - Remington 870 or 1100 shotgun, in either 12 gauge or 20 gauge
    - AR-15, from any American manufacturer, chambered in 5.56mm or .223 caliber
    - Marlin 336 rifle, in .30-30 caliber
    - Ruger 10/22, in .22 caliber (the only caliber that particular gun comes in.)

MONTH SEVEN

- Food for an additional one month.
- Study for ham radio technician class license. There are inexpensive study guides available. Ham radio can be an inexpensive hobby with tremendous preparedness applications.
- Exercise: continue with cardio and resistance training.

MONTH EIGHT

- Take a first aid class and get CPR certified.
- 500 rounds of premium grade, self-defense ammunition for the gun you purchased last month.
- Exercise: continue with cardio and resistance training.
- Continue to study for and successfully complete ham radio technician class license.
- Build a Bug Out Bag – a backpack containing three days' worth of food, water and essential supplies for every vehicle in your household to help you get home or to an area of safety in an emergency.
- Consumables: purchase six month's worth of toiletries and hygiene items.

MONTH NINE

- Alternative energy device – solar oven, solar generator, gasoline generator.
- Basic ham radio transmitter for 2 meter/70 centimeter band. Local ham radio operators in your community can help you get started with this.

MONTH TEN

- Training month. Spend one weekend doing the following:
  - Prepare all meals without using conventional cooking means.
  - Conduct family fire and tornado drills.
  - Bathe using alternative means at least once.
  - Practice using gear in bug out bags.
  - Practice using ham radio to make contacts. Determine what area ham radio repeaters are best suited for your neighborhood.
- Thoroughly debrief all training efforts. What worked well? What didn't? What extra items do you need to make your efforts more successful? What skills do you need to learn or practice?
- Health: If you have not had a check-up in the last two years, schedule one. If you have not seen your dentist or optometrist in the last year, schedule an appointment with them.
- Cash to cover an additional week's worth of living expenses.

MONTH ELEVEN

- Identify ways to develop a culture of preparedness in your workplace, school or neighborhood and start bringing them to fruition. See the examples in the prior chapters.
- Using your notes from last month's debriefing, determine when and how to get the extra training and supplies you need.
- Acquire a second firearm and a way to secure it, such as a lock box or gun safe if the one you purchased earlier in the year isn't large enough to accommodate both. This can either be another rifle or shotgun, or it can be a handgun. If you choose to acquire another rifle or shotgun, I highly recommend getting a clone of what you already have – the parts will be interchangeable in case one stops working. Purchasing a handgun if you don't have much experience with them

can be a daunting task, and everyone who has a handgun will have advice for you. As a firearms instructor who has taught a fair number of people – men and women, young and old, large and small - let me make it really easy for you. Just buy one of the guns off of the following list – and only this list - regardless of what the guy behind the gun counter (who isn't likely to be a NRA certified instructor) at your local gun store tells you:

- Glock 17 or 19 (both are chambered in 9 mm)
- Smith and Wesson M&P, chambered in 9mm
- Springfield XD, chambered in 9mm

MONTH TWELVE

- Where do you feel inadequate in your preparedness planning at the moment? Make any necessary purchases or attend training to help complete your preparedness efforts.
- Take a firearms training class to learn how to use your gun safely and effectively.

At this point, you should have:

- Approximately five months' worth of food
- Three weeks' worth of cash for living expenses
- Two months' worth of water (depending on the number of people you're planning for, you may not have enough space for this much water. Just do the best you can.)
- Two reliable firearms for self defense
- Alternative means to prepare food and generate power for recharging batteries and running small appliances
- First aid supplies and training
- Firearms training

- Your own project to help others get prepared at work or in the community
- A system to purify additional water you collect
- A ham radio license and basic radio to communicate with others during a disaster
- Completion of some preparedness drills around the house

Can you say you're absolutely, positively prepared for every emergency after doing all of these things? Of course not. But you will have established a good foundation upon which you can further build your level of preparedness. And it's safe to say you will have all of the things you need to ride out most emergencies you are likely to face. There will always be a helpful gadget, another month's worth of food, or a great training opportunity out there which will further enhance your level of readiness. How far you choose to go with it is up to you. Bear in mind you may be feeding and helping others, and not just your family. The more resources you have set aside will better enable you to be of help to others.

If every American had this level of preparedness, would we be a better country for it? Our fellow citizens would need a lot less in the way of FEMA debit cards and emergency meals. We would know when severe weather was approaching our area. Our neighborhoods would be safer if more people were adequately armed and trained to use their weapons. Our kids would know how to perform CPR.

Please don't let this intimidate you. Getting prepared is a journey. Start taking steps today to better prepare yourself and your family – no matter how small those steps are. And then keep taking steps. Keep getting better prepared. You strengthen yourself, your family, your community and your nation with every preparedness effort you make.

And please don't let the fear of making a mistake or doing something wrong deter you. You will make mistakes. Let me share some of mine with you.

PIVOT POINTS:

- A big part of effective apostleship for preparedness is being prepared ourselves. Many want to prepare but don't have a good idea where to start. It can be intimidating. Make sure you come up with a strategy that's sustainable.
- This will require some money. Figure out where you're not using money efficiently at the moment and use those funds to finance your preparedness efforts.
- Getting prepared isn't just about buying gear and other items. Knowing how to use it is critical. Don't overlook training and practice in your preparedness efforts.

ALPHA CHICKEN
DOG TWO-NINER

I have made many mistakes and had a few embarrassments in my own preparedness efforts. Once, while testing a damaged survival stove in my kitchen, it
burst into flames, resembling a little satellite upon re-entry into the earth's at-
mosphere. I managed to grab some kitchen tongs and take my Molotov cocktail
onto my front porch, where I promptly shot it with a fire extinguisher. A new
stove and a recharge on the fire extinguisher set me back about a hundred bucks.

Then there was the time my car battery died and, and despite having a bug
out bag and tool box, what I didn't have was – you guessed it – a set of jumper
cables. I had to call my wife to bring some from the house.

I've accidentally had live ammo in my coat pocket while going through airport security. I've relinquished some really nice knives and multi-tools at the
TSA checkpoint as well.

These things happen to those of us who try to be better prepared.

Then there have been the moments when others complained or made fun of
my efforts. My wife complains regularly that I am a high maintenance traveler,
as I seem to have lots of gear and gadgets with me at all times. I'll admit to carrying some odd things on our trips. I would also point out that these same gadgets – my multi-tool, flashlight, noise canceling headphones, external battery
for smart phones, Ziploc bags - seem to be in demand by her and other family
members when we travel.

My stepdaughter often makes fun of my efforts with my ham radio. One
evening a few years ago, after I unsuccessfully tried to contact someone –

anyone – on the radio, she started mimicking me as only a twelve year old can. She breathlessly told me and her mother "This is how you sound on the radio," cupping her hands up to her mouth to create some distortion in her voice. "*This is Alpha Chicken Dog Two-Niner, over.*"

Now I ask you: does my call sign, pronounced phonetically as *Kilo Delta Five Yankee Delta Mike* sound anything remotely close to *Alpha Chicken Dog Two Niner?* Of course not.

There's a tremendous amount of reluctance among Americans, even among those who think it's a priority, to engage in preparedness efforts. From talking to people from a wide variety of demographics, I sense the hesitancy stems from fear – fear of making a mistake and fear of being seen as someone who is crazy. No one wants to fail, nor do they want to be viewed as a paranoid nut job planning for an end of the world. Nor does anyone want to be an Alpha Chicken Dog Two Niner.

It's time to put those fears aside. It's time we became better citizens. The movement needs more leaders and doers who have the confidence to encourage others to join our effort. People are waking up to the reality that bad things can happen and that the government cannot take care of us when they do. Those people just need someone they trust to set an example and to help lead them with their next steps into readiness.

We have covered a lot of ground in the previous pages. I think it's helpful to provide you with an executive summary to help solidify what we've talked about in order to help you become the leaders our movement needs:

1. Americans want to be better prepared. They think it's a good investment, but they often lack the guidance and leadership on how to take those first steps.
2. Being interested in preparedness doesn't make you crazy. Psychology experts say that getting better prepared is mentally healthy and leads to a stronger sense of community.
3. There are a number of risks out there with which we must contend. Fortunately, preparing for one of them often helps prepare us for all of them.

4. Good preparedness is good citizenship.

5. For people of faith in the Abrahamic tradition, scripture exhorts us to be prepared.

6. Preparedness is not about winning. It's about putting yourself and family in a position to help others, to help rebuild, and to be a leader in the post-disaster environment.

7. Various government initiatives can help promote preparedness. We need to be objective when considering each of them to ensure that they will have the desired result in a cost effective manner.

8. Judicious ownership and use of firearms can help us avoid the effects of evil and provide a way to put food on the table during a crisis. Second Amendment advocates should make sure their advocacy efforts don't inadvertently discourage folks from getting into preparedness.

9. To create a culture of preparedness, we need to determine what such a culture would look like. We should study how others successfully changed the nation's culture and attitudes to determine if we can use those same strategies for our effort.

10. The most successful cultural change efforts in the past relied on one or more of the following strategies:

    a. Impressing the need for cultural change upon the youth

    b. Making the effort on a local level

    c. Utilizing tenets of a central faith and mobilizing the business community to take action

    d. Setting an expectation of readiness with consequences for compliance and failure

    e. Encouraging employers to make readiness among their employees a priority

11. No one will create a culture of preparedness for us. It will require us getting into our schools and communities, building relationships, and investing our own time and money into the effort. Sitting around hoping others do it for us is not an option.

12. To be a thought leader in the cultural change effort, we should not just increase our level of readiness. We should be a resource to others who want to learn more about preparedness as well as leading our own preparedness projects in our community. Don't be paralyzed by the size of the task. Start small and grow your efforts as your experience and confidence grow. Invite others to join the effort.

13. Preparedness is a journey. Most of us cannot get prepared with supplies and skills overnight. We are always learning new skills and strategies. We pay attention to the news and are up on current events. We know the next day's weather forecast. We keep ourselves in good physical shape.

14. Fear of failure and ridicule is the only thing that will derail this movement. No public interest group is going to lobby against our efforts to create a preparedness culture. The time is ripe to make major strides in the level of citizen readiness in America.

15. Patriots are called to serve their country selflessly. We should be willing to make a sacrifice of our time and resources in order to help create the change we want to see.

16. Find your pivot point to motivate you to create a culture of preparedness and then help others find theirs.

I don't measure the success of this book by the number of copies sold. I measure it by the number of people who are moved to take action to better ready themselves and their communities. So make a plan of action. What are you going to do to better prepare yourself? What project can you take on to better prepare your community?

Back in the introduction of the book, I wrote

Yet somewhere along the way, I clearly pivoted in my thought process. I realized the course I was on wasn't that helpful in the bigger scheme of things. It seemed wasteful of time, talent and energy for preppers to keep saying and doing the same things with some hope that people would join us in our efforts. The idea of staying the course no longer appealed to me. It became clear to me our movement needs to be on a different course – one where those in the movement are out in the community, helping others, setting a good example, being charitable, demonstrating good citizenship, and effectuating a culture change to incorporate preparedness strategies in our lives.

I don't want our movement to look back ten or twenty years from now, especially after some major disaster, and ask each other "what could we have done to prevent the problems people are experiencing because they weren't prepared?" I've had the privilege to meet a number of people who are actively preparing to improve their resilience. They are good hearted people with a willingness to help others. We need to expand that good nature and compassion for their fellow man into an advocacy force for the benefits of preparedness. We need those patriots who want to strengthen our nation's fabric to make creating a culture of preparedness an essential part of that strengthening.

In an earlier chapter, I discussed some of my preparedness service projects. As I was trying to get one of them off the ground, one of the people on the email distribution list asked me if I wasn't better off becoming what some preppers refer to as a "gray man" – someone who doesn't stand out, who preps quietly and without telling others. I assured them that I had thought of that and decided against it. Many may find prepping out in the open and encouraging others to do the same to be an unnecessary risk. Yet when I think back to those key moments in the early days of our country, we see the central thought leaders – people like Sam Adams, Paul Revere, John Hancock and George Washington - were not gray themselves. Nor were Martin Luther King, Jr., Rosa Parks, or Susan B. Anthony. They did not try to blend in. Instead, they inspired others to think and take action. While I don't put myself or my efforts on the same level as these great Americans, their leadership and commitment to a greater cause should inspire all of us to follow their example. Being a gray man or woman won't help improve our society.

So what will improve society and make us more resilient? People like you stepping up, getting better prepared, and leading your own initiative to encourage others. The road map to success has a number of different routes; the one you choose is up to you.

Find your pivot point. Choose your route. And then move forward. I promise you others will follow.

May the Lord bless us in our efforts.

Prepare now.

ENDNOTES

1. http://www.bestsellerblueprint.com/how-to-write-a-book/

2. http://www.huffingtonpost.com/2012/08/21/20-facts-hurricane-andrew-anniversary_n_1819405.html

3. http://www.wunderground.com/hurricane/damage.asp

4. *See* Romans 5:3-4

5. http://images.nationalgeographic.com/wpf/media-live/file/Doomsday_Preppers_Survey_-_Topline_Results.pdf

6. http://www.fema.gov/media-library-data/662ad7b4a323dcf07b829ce0c5b77ad9/2012+FEMA+National+Survey+Report.pdf

7. http://www.nhc.noaa.gov/pdf/TCR-AL092008_Ike_3May10.pdf

8. http://www.buzzfeed.com/emofly/hungry-new-york-families-dig-food-out-of-dumpsters

9. http://www.time.com/time/magazine/article/0,9171,1229102,00.html

10. Benson, Ragnar, *Survival End Game: The 21st Century Solution*. Paladin Press (2013) pg 21-22.

11. http://online.wsj.com/article/SB100014240529702041310045772376014071587 14.html
    see also http://www.ft.com/cms/s/0/9ff30d5c-be7d-11e3-a1bf-00144feabdc0.html#axzz2yQwdQivl

12. http://www.theguardian.com/world/2014/feb/17/time-to-join-preppers-survive-climate-change-apocalypse

13. Arbesman, Samuel, *The Half-Life of Facts; Why Everything We Know Has An Expiration Date.* Penguin Group (2012).

14. Id. at 29.

15. http://www.calculator.net/half-life-calculator.html?type=1&nt=&n0=1&t=14&t12=45&x=103&y=15

16. Jane Sinagub, email message to author, February 17, 2014.

17. Matt Davis, email message to author, August 11, 2014.

18. Id.

19. Id.

20. http://www.100resilientcities.org/cities/entry/san-franciscos-resilience-challenge#/-_/

21. http://online.wsj.com/articles/san-francisco-readies-for-the-big-one-a-block-at-a-time-1416443960

22. Id.

23. http://www.cdc.gov/homeandrecreationalsafety/fire-prevention/fires-factsheet.html

24. Id.

25. Id.

26. Id.

27. Calculated as follows: 0.37 x 2,640 = 976.8

28. http://www.ucar.edu/communications/factsheets/Flooding.html

29. Id.

30. http://www.heart.org/HEARTORG/CPRAndECC/WhatisCPR/
    CPRFactsandStats/CPR-Statistics_UCM_307542_Article.jsp

31. http://www.komonews.com/news/health/King-County-may-be-the-
    best-place-to-have-a-heart-attack-210592381.html?mobile=y

32. http://www.kingcounty.gov/healthservices/health/ems/community/
    aed/campaign.aspx

33. http://www.sja.org.uk/sja/about-us/latest-news/news-archive/news-
    stories-from-2010/april/2-in-3-couldnt-save-a-life.aspx

34. Id.

35. http://www.nfpa.org/research/reports-and-statistics/
    fires-by-property-type/residential/home-fires

36. Id.

37. http://www.nfpa.org/research/reports-and-statistics/
    fires-by-property-type/residential/home-fires

38. http://www.timesdispatch.com/news/myers-strong-building-codes-can-
    reduce-taxpayer-exposure/article_c92e89da-0a7a-54ed-86f7-
    e190086ec05f.html

39. http://www.cdc.gov/homeandrecreationalsafety/fire-prevention/fires-factsheet.html

40. http://www.sba.gov/content/disaster-planning

41. http://info.publicintelligence.net/FBI-SuspiciousActivity/Military_Surplus.pdf

42. https://www.youtube.com/watch?v=_cleZRshEw4

43. Genesis 6:9. Unless otherwise indicated, all biblical citations are from the New Living Translation.

44. Genesis 6:18

45. Genesis 6:14 – 16

46. Genesis 6:19 – 21

47. Genesis 7:4; 7:10

48. Genesis 9:1

49. *See* Genesis 22:14

50. Genesis 41:33 – 36

51. Genesis 39:2

52. Genesis 41:16

53. Genesis 45: 4 – 5

54. Nehemiah 4:15-18

55. Nehemiah 7: 3

56. Luke 22:35-37

57. John 2:13-16

58. *See* John 16:25

59. Matthew 25:1-13

60. Matthew 25:14-30

61. Matthew 24: 36-44

62. Matthew 25:35-40

63. 1 John 3:17-18

64. Rawles, James Wesley, *How to Survive the End of The World As We Know It.* Penguin Group (2009), pg. 16.

65. Id.

66. Matthew 6:34

67. Matthew 6:33

68. http://www.mormonnewsroom.org/facts-and-stats

69. http://www.mormonnewsroom.org/facts-and-statistics

70. https://www.lds.org/topics/emergency-preparedness

71. https://www.lds.org/topics/emergency-preparedness

72. Benson, Ezra Taft, *The Teachings of Ezra Taft Benson*. Bookcraft (1988), pg. 263-264.

73. Id.

74. Psalm 23:4

75. http://www.cnn.com/2005/US/09/03/katrina.chertoff/

76. http://www.nola.com/hurricane/content.ssf?/washingaway/thebigone_1.html

77. http://reason.com/archives/2005/09/10/defenseless-on-the-bayou

78. http://www.foxnews.com/story/2006/04/19/no-police-returning-guns-confiscated-post-katrina/

79. http://www.txdps.state.tx.us/LawEnforcementSupport/texas1033.htm

80. http://reason.com/archives/2010/05/11/a-drug-raid-goes-viral

81. http://www.constitution.org/abus/le/miac-strategic-report.pdf

82. http://www.scribd.com/doc/49313711/Apology-for-miac-report

83. http://www.breitbart.com/Big-Government/2013/04/04/The-Great-DHS-Ammunition-Stockpile-Myth

84. http://www.breitbart.com/Big-Government/2013/04/04/ The-Great-DHS-Ammunition-Stockpile-Myth

85. *Mark G.A.Welsh, a minor, and Elliott A.Welsh, his father and next friend, Plaintiffs-Appellants, v. Boy Scouts of America and Boy Scouts of America West Suburban Council # 147, Defendants-Appellees*, 993 F.2d 1267 (1993).

86. James 2:1-7

87. Leviticus 19:15

88. 28 U.S.C § 453

89. Lee, Dr. Richard G. and Countryman, Jack, *God's Promises for the American Patriot*. Thomas Nelson Publishers (2011), pg. 8.

90. FreedomWorks, *Rules for Patriots*, pg. 4

91. Lee, Dr. Richard G. and Countryman, Jack, *God's Promises for the American Patriot*. Thomas Nelson Publishers (2011), pg. 8

92. http://www.revenue.louisiana.gov/sections/Publications/ HurricanePrepSalesTaxHoliday.aspx;see also http://revenue.louisiana.gov/ sections/general/hottopics/secondamendment.aspx

93. http://taxfoundation.org/article/sales-tax-holidays-politically-expedient-poor-tax-policy-2014

94. Id.

95. http://taxfoundation.org/blog/virginias-hurricane-sales-tax-holiday

96. http://www.fte.org

97. http://www.fte.org/teacher-resources/lesson-plans/disasterslessons/lesson-3-when-disaster-strikes-what-can-government-do/

98. http://www.fte.org/teacher-resources/lesson-plans/disasterslessons/lesson-3-when-disaster-strikes-what-can-government-do/

99. https://www.disastersafety.org/wp-content/uploads/IBHS-Rating-the-States-2015.pdf

100. https://www.disastersafety.org/wp-content/uploads/rating-the-states-midterm-chart-2013.jpg

101. *See*, "Rating the States – An Assessment of Residential Building Code and Enforcement Systems for Life Safety and Property Protection in Hurricane-Prone Regions," (December 2011), pg. 3

102. 42 USC 5121 *et seq.*

103. 42 USC 5121(b)(1)-(6)

104. Mulitihazard Mitigation Council, *NATURAL HAZARD MITIGATION SAVES: An Independent Study to Assess the Future Savings from Mitigation Activities*, Volume 2 – Study Documentation, (2005), pg. 123-139.

105. In full disclosure, my employer, the National Association of Mutual Insurance Companies, has been an ardent supporter of this legislation.

106. http://buildstrongamerica.com/issue/

107. The Disaster Savings Accounts Act, H.R. 3989, 113th Congress. In full disclosure, my employer, the National Association of Mutual Insurance Companies, has been an ardent supporter of this legislation.

108. In full disclosure, my employer, the National Association of Mutual Insurance Companies, has been an ardent supporter of this legislation.

109. http://www.forbes.com/sites/anthonynitti/2013/10/17/would-you-prepare-your-home-for-a-disaster-if-it-were-tax-deductible/

110. https://www.lp.org/files/2014_LP_Platform.pdf

111. http://www.lp.org/news/press-releases/lp-chair-to-washington-stop-destroying-jobs-so-the-economy-can-grow.

112. http://www.economist.com/blogs/democracyinamerica/2012/01/libertarians

113. http://www.businessweek.com/articles/2012-12-27/how-often-do-we-use-guns-in-self-defense

114. 100,000 DGUs per year divided by 365 days a year equals 273.97 DGUs per day.

115. 370,000 DGUs per year divided by 365 days a year equals 1,013.69 DGUs per day. 1,013 DGUs per day divided by 24 hours equals 42.23 DGUs per hour.

116. http://www.npr.org/templates/story/story.php?storyId=5640177

117. 8 C.F.R. 337.1

118. 5 U.S.C. §3331

119. http://www.history.army.mil/html/faq/oaths.html

120. Hunt, Swanee, *This Was Not Our War: Bosnian Women Reclaiming The Peace.* Duke University Press, (2004).

121. http://abcnews.go.com/Blotter/exclusive-westgate-interpol-chief-ponders-armed-citizenry/story?id=20637341

122. Douglass, Frederick, *Life and Times of Frederick Douglass, Written by Himself.* De Wolfe & Fiske Co. (1892), pg. 460.

123. http://georgewbush-whitehouse.archives.gov/reports/katrina-lessons-learned/chapter6.html

124. Honore', Russel L, and Martz, Ron, *Survival – How Being Prepared Can Keep You And Your Family Safe.* Simon and Schuster (2009), pg. 6.

125. http://www.emergencymgmt.com/disaster/Creating-a-Culture-of.html

126. http://www.whitehouse.gov/blog/2012/01/19/creating-culture-preparedness

127. http://www.cdc.gov/features/vitalsigns/adultsmoking/

128. http://www.cdc.gov/nchs/data/databriefs/db89.htm

129. http://www.newyorker.com/magazine/2013/04/15/when-the-earth-moved

130. http://www.examiner.com/article/new-study-finds-a-decrease-school-bullying-the-u-s

131. http://www.cdc.gov/features/vitalsigns/adultsmoking/

132. http://www.crisisprevention.com/Resources/Article-Library/Nonviolent-Crisis-Intervention-Training-Articles/10-Ways-to-Help-Reduce-Bullying-in-Schools

133. http://www.npr.org/2014/03/30/296441067/what-a-small-towns-teen-pregnancy-turnaround-can-teach-the-u-s?utm_medium=facebook&utm_source=npr&utm_campaign=nprnews&utm_content=03302014

134. http://www.newyorker.com/magazine/2013/04/15/when-the-earth-moved

135. http://www.newyorker.com/magazine/2013/04/15/when-the-earth-moved

136. http://www.newyorker.com/magazine/2013/04/15/when-the-earth-moved

137. $3 a day multiplied by 365 days a year equals $1,095 in additional payments. Multiplying that figure by 30 years results in an additional $32,850.

138. http://www.ready.gov/business

139. http://www.ready.gov/workplace-plans

140. http://www.mdcinc.org/sites/default/files/resources/When%20Disaster%20Strikes%20-%20Promising%20Practices%20-%20Low-Income%20Families%20and%20Communities.pdf, citing Vatsa, K. (2004). Risk, Vulnerability, and Asset-based Approach to Disaster Risk Management. International Journal of Sociology and Social Policy, 24(10/11).

141. http://usatoday30.usatoday.com/news/nation/story/2012-03-11/tornado-mobile-homes/53477486/1

142. http://www.austinfoodbank.org/how-we-help/disaster-preparedneses-and-relief.html

143. http://www.americaslibrary.gov/jb/modern/jb_modern_selma_1.html

144. http://www.earthday.org/earth-day-history-movement

145. http://www.tcnj.edu/~borland/2006-aids/cassy2.htm, citing Smith, Raymond A., Ed. *The Encyclopedia of AIDS: A Social, Political, Cultural, and Scientific Record of the HIV Epidemic.*. Fitzroy Dearborn Publishers (1998), pg 36.

146. Exodus 4: 10-16

147. http://hirr.hartsem.edu/research/fastfacts/fast_facts.html

148. http://www.hopkinsmedicine.org/news/media/releases/johns_hopkins_experts_to_develop_fema_training_model_for_disaster_response_by_churches_and_other_houses_of_worship